RECOLLECTIONS OF ROSSETTI

RECOLLECTIONS OF ROSSETTI

Hall Caine

Dante Gabriel Rossetti was living in seclusion in Chelsea when an aspiring young writer, Hall Caine, came to see him and to hear his story.

Rossetti's wife, Lizzie Siddal, who had been spotted working in a milliner's shop in Oxford Street by one of Rossetti's friends, was the archetypal pre-Raphaelite beauty, and a model for much of Rossetti's work. She languished on the pedestal on which he had set her, and, falling into a depression after the birth of a still-born baby, she eventually died of an overdose of laudanum.

Grief stricken, Rossetti wrapped a volume of his poems in his dead wife's red-gold hair and buried it with her. But seven years later, believing it to have been his best written work, he had her exhumed in order to recover it. Subsequently, and during the time Caine knew him, he became depressed and guilt-ridden. Believing he was cursed for his desecration of his wife's grave, he too fell into a decline, becoming dependent on opiates.

Hall Caine gives an extraordinarily strong impression of what it was like to meet Rossetti and to share a home with him in the last few months of his life. He tells this sad story with the under-standing of a close friend, and the reader cannot but be moved by the account, in the final pages, of the great man dying in Hall Caine's arms.

RECOLLECTIONS
OF
ROSSETTI

by

Hall Caine

with an introduction by Jan Marsh

CENTURY
London Sydney Auckland Johannesburg

Copyright Introduction © Jan Marsh 1990

First published in Great Britain in 1928 by Cassell & Company Ltd
Reissued 1990 by Century
An imprint of Random Century Ltd
20 Vauxhall Bridge Road, London SW1V 2SA

CENTURY HUTCHINSON AUSTRALIA (PTY) LTD
20 Alfred Street, Milsons Point, Sydney, NSW 2061, Australia

Century Hutchinson New Zealand Ltd
PO Box 40-086, 32-34 View Road, Glenfield, Auckland 10, New Zealand

Century Hutchinson South Africa (Pty) Ltd
PO Box 337, Bergvlei 2012, South Africa

Set in Garamond Original by SX Composing Ltd, Rayleigh, Essex
Printed and bound in Great Britain by
The Guernsey Press Co. Ltd, Guernsey, Channel Islands
British Library Cataloguing in Publication data

Caine, hall, 1853-1931
Recollections of Rossetti. – (National Trust classics)
1. English paintings. Rossetti, Dante Gabriel, 1828-1882
I. Title II. Series
759.2

ISBN 0-7126-3730-3

I DEDICATE
THIS BOOK TO THE MEMORY
OF A GREAT FRIENDSHIP
1879-1928

CONTENTS

INTRODUCTION

"One of the most rarely gifted men of our time has just died" proclaimed the *Athenaeum* when the death of Dante Gabriel Rossetti was announced in April 1882. Yet for many years Rossetti had been 'the most retired man of genius of our day', never seen in public, and known only through his published poetry and (seldom exhibited) painting.

Through his art, Rossetti was famed as lover and worshipper of woman's beauty in what is now seen as the typical Pre-Raphaelite mode – swan-necked, heavy-lidded women with lavish hair and compelling gaze. The reclusive private life and the rumours that whispered as to its cause fed a demand for biographical studies and personal reminiscences of this great, if mysteriously flawed, Romantic genius. And within six months of his death, a slim volume of recollections issued from the pen of young Thomas Hall Caine, who had befriended the artist in his last, troubled years. In 1928, the centenary of Rossetti's birth, this was revised and re-issued under the present title.

Today, Rossetti is best known as the leading light of the Pre-Raphaelite Brotherhood or PRB of 1848, for his still striking images of women, and for his personal relations with his models – Elizabeth Siddal (later his wife), Janey Morris, Fanny Cornforth and the rest. This is as recounted here in Chapter 3, summarising Rossetti's life as the 'genial and masterful' king of his circle until his wife's tragic death from an overdose. According to Caine this loss – and the still more terrible exhumation of Lizzie's coffin to retrieve Rossetti's notebook – marked the start of the decline that clouded the remainder of the artist's life, darkened by delusions and drug-taking. It was, however, the period of his most admired poems, including the House of Life sonnet sequence, which were first published in 1870 and the subject of a fierce attack (on their morality not prosody) which triggered a catastrophic mental breakdown from which Rossetti never truly recovered. Hence, in large part, the seclusion of his last years.

Hall Caine (1853-1931) who gives a brief but sufficient account of his own origins here, was a callow but ambitious young man in Liverpool when in a local lecture he defended the moral tenor of Rossetti's verse – as in the much-maligned poem about a student's visit to a prostitute that begins

> Lazy laughing languid Jenny,
> Fond of a kiss and fond of a guinea,
> Whose head upon my knee tonight
> Rests for a while . . .

He sent the text of his lecture to Rossetti, who responded warmly. Indeed, Rossetti's letters to Caine, now in the Manx Museum, are worthy of publication. They deal chiefly with matters poetic: Keats, Coleridge, Blake, Chatterton, Donne, Smart, Milton,

Shakespeare.

Through their epistolary friendship, Caine went on to help the city of Liverpool negotiate the purchase of Rossetti's large painting *Dante's Dream on the Anniversary of the Death of Beatrice* (now in the Walker Art Gallery).

His hero-worship was rewarded when he was invited to lodge with Rossetti in Tudor House on Cheyne Walk, in what proved the last months of the artist's life. Rossetti was without doubt deranged; from the symptoms of unfounded paranoia and acute mental agitation, it is my belief that he suffered from some form of schizophrenia, in which lucid opinions alternated with insane delusions and those who disagreed were taken for enemies or, in Rossetti's words, false summer friends. Although attributing the malady to chloral (in actuality a sedative strong enough to quell the agitation for a few hours) Caine's text supports this interpretation. Appalled and fascinated by Rossetti's behaviour, he was innocent enough to hope that he could help, and his account of Rossetti's visit to Cumberland in autumn 1881, the return to London and the final weeks, gives a vivid, tragic and moving picture of the end. Rossetti died of kidney failure in a borrowed bungalow in Birchington, Kent, at the age of 53.

From the grave of the dead, tormented genius grew a thriving biographical and mythological industry, of which Caine was by no means the only beneficiary. On his reputation as the man in whose arms Rossetti had died he built a solid literary career in fiction and criticism. Although his name is now virtually unknown and his work unread, he prospered, with some thirty titles to his credit; in 1918 he was knighted and later retired to the Isle of Man.

His gratitude and reverence for Rossetti never faded, and when 1928 saw several centenary biographies (one from the young Evelyn Waugh) Caine was prompted to re-issue his *Recollections*, adding much that would have been impossible or ill-advised to publish in 1882, or in 1908 when the story was re-told in Caine's autobiography. Most sensationally, this related (in Chapter 12) to Elizabeth Siddal's death – said by the coroner to be an accident but widely remoured to be intentional – and the train journey when Rossetti confided to Caine that he had found a suicide note by his wife's bed.

The truth of this cannot be ascertained. As he himself admits on page three, Caine was not renowned for veracity. But it adds a thrillingly Gothick touch to an evocative and well-told tale, illuminating Rossetti's last months and illustrating why his life as well as his art still exerts such a powerful fascination over our imaginations. Sadly, although there are several monographs on his work currently in print, the last substantial biography of Rossetti was published in 1949.

A few items in the text may require explanation. The poet friend who lost his hair on page 47 was William Bell Scott, better known as an artist. The man who called Rossetti an 'animal' (i.e. sensual) painter on page 79 was the Liverpool collector and patron Harold Rathbone (whom Rossetti in his paranoia dubbed 'Ratsbane'). The 'bouncing girl' cracking nuts in Vauxhall Gardens on page 110 was Fanny Cornforth, then a prostitute, later Rossetti's model and mistress – 'a raging red-haired trollop' according to

Bernard Shaw – and also the so-called 'nurse' in Cumberland who on page 121 revealed Caine's subterfuge with the chloral, and the 'old friend' after whom Rossetti inquired on his death-bed.

Rossetti's other *inamorata*, the dark-browed Janey Morris, was visible only in his paintings – for when, once or twice, she visited Cheyne Walk in the last months, Caine was not introduced. But he hinted at the then-secret love affair as 'a great passion coming too late', implying that more might be revealed.

Early in their friendship, Rossetti remarked on Caine's 'overloaded' literary style. It remained so to the end: inwrought, luxuriant, suggestive, with a taste for the purple. Yet his narrative talent as a story-teller was and is consummate. Take a pinch of salt, and read on.

© JAN MARSH 1990

Jan Marsh is a biographer and critic and author of *Pre-Raphaelite Sisterhood* (1985) and *The Legend of Elizabeth Siddal* (1989).

AUTHOR'S NOTE

On the recent occasion of Rossetti's centenary many evil things were published in important places about him and about the friends of his later years. I am, and have long been, the last of Rossetti's friends surviving, all others claiming that name being no more than his friendly acquaintances. I felt that I had a right to reply, but I did not do so. Grave circumstances compelled me then to be silent. and now I am not, I trust, the man to let resentment go beyond the grave.

But I have still my duty to the dead, and in this book I have endeavoured, with all simplicity, to discharge it. I possess the largest body of Rossetti's literary and personal letters that exists or has ever existed. For a considerable period I was his housemate. When his last illness fell upon him I was with him every day – nearly all day and often all night. He died in my arms. The first word that was said about him in print after his death was said by me. Therefore I believe myself to be the earliest and only reliable authority on the period of his later life. My credentials come from Rossetti himself.

In this book I have made no reply to the authors of the evil things that have been said about Rossetti and his friends. I have left the story of their devoted friendship to speak for itself. I strive with none. On this subject I feel that "none are worth my strife."

Thus I have tried to snatch back a little of the lost grace of a day which I had hoped would be a day of rejoicing for the birth of a great soul into the world.

H. C.

Isle of Man.

RECOLLECTIONS OF ROSSETTI

CHAPTER I

HOW I CAME TO KNOW ROSSETTI

In my youth I was apprenticed to an architect in Liverpool, but as early as my seventeenth year I fell a victim to the nervous disorders which have been the greatest disability of my life, and I was sent back for a time to my father's family in the Isle of Man. During this period I lived first with my grandmother in a little thatched cotage on the high road through one of the remote parts of the island. Later I lived with an uncle by marriage, who was a schoolmaster in a schoolhouse that stood alone like a lighthouse on the bleakest of the Manx headlands, where the wind in winter swirled round it and lashed it as with a knout, and the sea-gulls, driven helpless before the fury of a storm, would sometimes crash through the window-panes.

My uncle died, and in some informal way I took his place in schoolmastering, with all the extraneous duties that pertained to it, such as the making of wills for the farmers round about, the drafting of agreements and leases, the writing of letters to banks complaining against crushing interest, and occasionally the inditing of love-letters for young farm-hands to their girls in service on farms that were far away.

There was still another side to my occupations.

Being cut off from my T-square and drawing board, I began to read and, after a while, to write. My books were at first confined to such as were kept on the "laff" (the ceiling-shelf in the kitchen), the bible and "Pilgrim's Progress" and "Clark's Commentaries" and "The Land and the Book." I had few books of poetry and I had none of fiction, for what we afterwards called the Nonconformist conscience had already penetrated our bleak solitude and our seniors had no place for the authors who (as an unforgiving Manxman in later years said of myself) "earned their living by telling lies".

This was about 1870, and through the thick mists of my moorland home there came (I cannot remember how) the rumour that a poet of Italian name, Dante Gabriel Rossetti, had published a volume of poems. We did not see his poems, and therefore we did not read them, but a story of how they came to be published began to be common talk among us. It was the tragic story of how the original manuscript had been buried in the coffin of the poet's wife and then exhumed after lying seven years in the grave. I remember that a thrill came to me with that story, and then, close behind it, a sense of outrage, as if the grace of a great renunciation had been finally thrown away.

I got better for a time and returned to my architect's office in Liverpool. There, or at some period a little later, in a literary society which I had founded, I made the acquaintance of a Liverpool journalist, named Ashcroft Noble, who was an enthusiastic admirer of Rossetti's poems, and, through him, of a boy still younger than myself, very slight and pale, and reminding me constantly of Keats – not alone by his poetic gifts, but also by his physical weakness, for he was then very delicate. This was William Watson, now Sir William Watson, also an enthusiastic admirer of Rossetti's poems, and himself destined to become a poet and, I am sure, a great one.

Not long after this, by reason of an essay called "The Supernatural in Poetry", which I had published in the magazine that had once been sub-edited by George Eliot, I made the acquaintance of H. A. Bright, the "H. A. B." of Hawthorne's letters and his closest friend during his Consulate in Liverpool. Through Bright I came to know Lord Houghton, the biographer of Keats and the father of the present Marquis of Crewe, and through both of these I came to hear more of Rossetti and of the grim story of the buried book.

Bright had known something of Rossetti, and, in reply to my eager questioning, he told me that the poet was a little dark man (little he was not), with fine eyes under a broad brow – a little Italian, in short. I think it was Lord Houghton who said that Rossetti, in the days when he used to meet him at Mrs. Gaskell's, was a young fellow of strong bohemian habits (meaning thereby, I presumed, a certain tendency to recklessness and even indecorum) and that he was known at that time principally as a painter and the leader of an eccentric school of art, but also as a poet, whose poems were much belauded by a narrow circle, of which Swinburne was the most vocal and vehement.

I recall that on a holiday in the Lake country some years later, I quenched my thirst for every sort of *ana* relating to Rossetti from a stranger whom I thought I recognized as the author of "Festus". I heard from him that in his young manhood Rossetti's manners had been, to say the least, robustious, suggesting a person in deliberate revolt against nearly all the conventions of society, and delighting, if only out of perversity or for devilish amusement, in every opportunity to startle well-ordered people out of their propriety by championing the worst view of Neronian Rome, and by silencing, by sheer vehemence of denunciation, the seemly protests of very good and gentle folk.

But more arresting, because obviously of more serious import than such pictures of the excesses of a vigorous physical and intellectual youth, were the slight peeps I was able to get from Bright, Houghton, and others of the life the poet lived then. It appeared that Rossetti had long been living in the strictest seclusion in a large house in Chelsea, which had once been the home of the Princess Elizabeth; that neither the literary nor the artistic society of London saw anything of him; that his face was unknown to the pictorial newspapers and unfamiliar to his contemporaries in either of the two arts in which he was now illustrious; that outside a close and very limited circle he was as one who was dead and buried save for the splendid achievements in poetry and painting which emerged at intervals from the sealed doors of his tomb.

It was natural that about an existence so shrouded by mystery various myths should have gathered, and in reply to my questioning I received a number of fragmentary romances, some of them having, as I now see, a certain substratum of truth. Thus I was told that Rossetti's seclusion had been due to the shock occa-

sioned by the death of his wife; and again, to the remorse that had followed on having allowed himself to
exhume her body for the recovery of the manuscripts
which he had buried in her grave; and yet again, to the
distress and sense of degradation which had resulted
upon the adverse criticism of a brother-poet, taken up
by a whole pack of critical hounds in full cry.

Such were the portraits of Rossetti with which I fed
my curiosity in those early days in Liverpool, and the
first outcome of my enthusiasm was a lecture which I
delivered at the local Free Library. The text of that lecture I have long ago lost, but as it probably gave birth
to the friendship which it will be my duty and pleasure
to describe, I shall perhaps be doing well to trust to
my memory in an effort to indicate its drift.

I do not remember to have said anything about Rossetti the man, though that might have been a promis-
ing theme for a popular audience, neither did I attempt
to tell the story of the origin and publication of his
books, but I gave a narrative account of the stories of
his greater poems, and then wound up with an abstract
analysis of the impulses animating his work. In this
analysis I argued that to place Rossetti amongst the
"aesthetic" poets was an error of classification; that he
had nothing in common with the Caliban of Browning, who worked "for work's sole sake"; that the top-
most thing in him was indeed love of beauty, but the
deepest thing was love of truth, often plain and un-
comely truth; that the fusion of these two passions
had at the same time softened the Italian Catholic,
which I recognized as a leading element in him, and
purified the Italian troubadour; that while he was too
true an artist to follow art into its byeways of moral

significance and so cripple its broader aims, the absorption of the artist in his art seemed always to live and work together with the personal instincts of the man; that to do good on the other grounds was, in Rossetti's art, involved and included in being good on its own; that the manner of doing a thing could never be more than a part of a thing done, and that the most unmoral of all poetry – Poe's, for example – involved many meanings, purposes, and results; that Rossetti's poetry showed how possible it was, without making conscious compromise with that Puritan principle of "doing good" of which Keats had been enamoured, to be unconsciously making for moral ends; and finally, that there was a passive Puritanism in "Jenny," and in the most ardent of the sonnets, which lived and worked together with the poet's artistic passion for doing his work supremely well.

I cannot but smile when I cast my mind back some fifty years and think of myself as a young fellow of five-and-twenty, full to the throat of the last phrase, not to say the last jargon, of the "higher" literary criticism, pouring out its abstract theories to an audience consisting chiefly of working men and women, who listened to me, I remember, in the most indulgent silence. But sure I am that some kindly fate must have been directing my incongruous efforts, for knowing Rossetti's nature as I afterwards learned to know it, I see that such pleading for the moral influences animating his work was of all things most likely to enlist his sympathy and engage his affections. Smarting still under the monstrous accusation that he had, by his poetry, been engaged with others in an attempt to demoralize the public mind of the glorification of mere lust, he jumped with eagerness at a whole-hearted defence of his literary and human impulses, as a writer who had been prompted by the highest of spiritual emotions, and as a man to whom the passions of the body were as nothing unless sanctified by the concurrence of the soul.

My lecture was printed about a year after its delivery, and then, eagerly but nervously, and I think modestly, I sent a copy of it to the poet, hardly expecting more than a word of response. A post of two later brought me, however, the following reply:

16, CHEYNE WALK, CHELSEA.
29th July, 1879.

DEAR MR. CAINE, – I am much struck by the generous enthusiasm displayed in your lecture, and by the ability with which it is written. Your estimate of the impulses influencing my poetry is such as I could wish it to suggest, and this suggestion, I believe, it will always have for a true-hearted nature. You say that you are grateful to me; my response is that I am grateful to you, for you have spoken up heartily and unfalteringly for the work you love.

I daresay you sometimes come to London. I should be very glad to know you, and would ask you, if you thought of calling, to give me a day's notice when to expect you, as I am not always able to see visitors without appointment. The afternoon about 5 might suit me, or else the evening about 9.30.

With all best wishes, yours sincerely,

D. G. ROSSETTI.

CHAPTER II

THE BEGINNING OF A GREAT

FRIENDSHIP

If the foregoing letter seems to the reader to be little more than a courteous acknowledgment by a famous poet of an appreciative criticism sent by a stranger, I must urge that, in order to realize what it meant to me, it is necessary to think of who and what I was, as (for this purpose, chiefly) I have tried to show myself in the foregoing story – a young man in the country who had begun life in the most unlikely of all conditions for the pursuit of the literary calling; who had scratched and scrambled through a kind of miscellaneous education, heaven knows how; who had made efforts to emerge from an environment for which he was quite unfit and thus far failed in all of them. To this raw and untutored beginner, quite unrecognized and unknown, a great man, illustrious in two arts, in return for a little essay, a mere lecture delivered in a provincial city to an audience whose opinion could have no sensible effect on his fame, held out his hand and said, at a moment perhaps of deep discouragement, "I should be very glad to know you." Is it a matter for much surprise that the day I received that first letter from Rossetti seemed to me to be the greatest day of my life?

I think it not improbable that my reply sufficiently expressed the emotion I describe, for the poet wrote to me again and again within a very few days, with a warmth and tenderness which I still feel to be, under the circumstances of the great disparity between us, both as to age and gifts and condition, almost inexpressibly touching.

"My dear Caine," he wrote, after a while, "let me assure you at once that correspondence with yourself is one of my best pleasures, and that you cannot write too much or too often for *me*; though after what you have told me as to the apportioning of your time" (I had to be at my office at six in the morning in those days), "I would be unwilling to encroach unduly upon it. Neither should I, on my side, prove very tardy in reply, as you are one to whom I find there is something to say when I sit down with a pen and paper. I have a good deal of enforced evening leisure, as it is seldom I can paint or draw by gaslight. It would not be right in me to refrain from saying that to meet with one so 'leal and true' to myself as you are has been a consolation amid much discouragement.

Do please drop the 'Mr.' in writing to me again."

Thus far Rossetti knew nothing more about me than I have indicated in this narrative, but he was naturally curious to learn something about his correspondent, and in those early days he put pointed questions occasionally.

"Someone to whom I showed your article," he wrote, "would insist, from the last paragraph, that you must be a Roman Catholic. Is this the case? Pardon my putting the query, as I perceive, rather abruptly."

On this hint I wrote freely enough, apparently, and he replied:

"I am truly delighted to hear how young you are: I suppose you are not married. In original work a man does some of his best things by your time of life, though he only finds it out in a rage much later, at some date when he expected to know no longer that he had ever done them. Keats did not die so much too early if there was any danger of his taking to the modern habit eventually of treating material as product, and shooting it all out as it comes. Of course, however, he wouldn't; he was getting always choicer and simpler; my favourite piece in his works is 'La Belle Dame sans Merci' – I suppose about his last. As to Shelley, it is really a mercy that he has not been hatching yearly universes till now. He might, I suppose; for his friend Trelawney still walks the earth without greatcoat, stockings, or underclothing this Christmas (1879).

"In criticism, matters are very different as to the seasons of production, though you have done work already that should honour you yet. Nothing strikes me about you to better purpose than your simple lucidity, where that alone is wanted, as in the lecture you sent me.

"I am writing hurriedly and horridly in every sense. Write again, and I'll try and answer better. All greetings to you."

Again, he wrote: "The comparative dates of our births are curious (I myself was born on old May Day ('12') in the year (1828) after that in which Blake died.) ... You were born, in fact, just as I was giving up poetry, at about 25, on finding that it impeded attention to what constituted another aim and a livelihood into the bargain, i.e. painting. From that date, up to the year when I published my poems, I wrote extremely little – I might almost say nothing, except the renovated 'Jenny' in 1858 or '59. To this again I added a passage or two when publishing in 1870."

My employment in Liverpool delayed for many months the moment when I was to meet Rossetti in London, but our intimacy deepened by correspondence, and he began to send me some of the shorter poems which he had not yet published, and to ask me to show him such work as I had done myself.

"Tell me what you think of my things," he said. "All you said in your letter this morning was very grateful to me. I have a fair amount by me in the way of later MS., which I may show some day when we meet. Meantime I feel that your energies are already in full swing – work coming on the heels of work – and that your time cannot be long delayed as regards your place as a writer. Do you write poetry? I should think you must surely do so."

In replies to inquiries like this I was naturally very eager to show what I had done; so I sent poetry, criticism, prose narrative, and, I think, fragments of drama, most of it unpublished, and some of it never to see print.

"I return your article on the 'Supernatural in Poetry,'" he said. "In reading it I feel it a distinction that my minute plot in the poetic field should have attracted the gaze of one who is able to traverse its widest ranges with so much command. I shall be much pleased if the plan of calling on me is carried out soon – at any rate, I trust it will be so eventually.

I have been reading again your article on the 'Supernatural.' It is truly admirable; such work must soon make you a place. The dramatic paper" (it was a phamphlet on Henry Irving's Macbeth) "I thought suffered from some immaturity; moreover, if I were you, I should eschew modern dramatic matters."

"I perceive," he wrote playfully, "you have had a complete poetic career, which you have left behind to strike out into wider waters! The passage on 'Night', which you say was written under the planet Shelley, seems to me (and to my brother, to whom I read it) to savour more of the 'mortal moon' – that is, of a weird and sombre Elizabethanism, of which Beddoes may be considered the modern representative. But we both think it has an unmistakable force and value; and if you can write better poetry than this, let your angel say unto you – *Write*."

But Rossetti's critical indulgence of the youngest of poetasters did not forbid the expression of a frank opinion. "You may be sure," he said, "I do not mean essential discouragement when I say that, full as 'Nell' is of reality and pathos, your swing of arm seems to me firmer and freer in prose than in verse. You know already how high I rate your future career (short of the incalculable storms of Fate), but I do think I see your field to lie chiefly in the noble achievements of fervid and impassioned prose . . . I thought the passage on 'Night' showed an aptitude for choice imagery. I should much like to see something which you view as your best poetic effort hitherto. After all, there is no need that every gifted writer should take the path of poetry. I am confident in your preference for frankness on my part."

While the hampering conditions of my employment delayed our coming together, Rossetti showed a good deal of friendly anxiety to bring me into contact with such of his friends as were near to Liverpool or had occasion to visit it. In this way I met Madox Brown, and sat to him for one of the figures in his admirable frescoes in the Town Hall at Manchester; and in this way, too, I met Stephens, the art critic.

"I am very glad you were welcomed by dear staunch Stephens, on his visit to your Royal Institution, as I felt sure you would be. He is one of my oldest and best friends, of whom few can be numbered at my age, from causes only too varying –

> Go from me, summer friends, and tarry not –
> I am no summer friend, but wintry cold.

"So be it, as needs must be – not for all, let us hope, and not *with* all, as good Stephens shows. I have not seen him since his return. I wrote him a line to thank him for his friendly reception of you, and he wrote in return to thank *me* for your acquaintance, and spoke very pleasantly of you. Your youth seems to have surprised him. . . . You mention something he said to you of me and my surroundings. They are certainly *quiet* enough as far as retirement goes, and I have often thought I should enjoy the presence of a congenial and intellectual house-fellow and board-fellow in this big barn of mine, which is actually going to rack and ruin for want of use. But where to find the welcome, the willing and the able combined in one? . . . Your letter holds out the welcome probability of meeting you here ere long."

This note of his loneliness was only too insistent in

his earlier letters. "I am sometimes very solitary," he said, "and then letter-writing brings solace, when one addresses so young and hopeful a well-wisher as yourself. Accordingly I sit down to-night to answer your last letter."

My health failed me for a time, and though Rossetti and I had not even yet seen each other face to face, his anxiety about my condition could not have been greater had I been his own son.

"You are very young to be so beset with dark moods," he said, "and I am much concerned to hear it. Everyone, I suppose, thinks *he* only knows the full bitterness of the Shadowed Valley. I hope health is whole with you – then all *must* come out well, with your mind and such energy as yours to make its way. It is very late – good-bye for to-night."

Such were the earliest of the letters which formed the beginnings of my first great literary friendship, and if I have permitted myself to transcribe the too generous words of one whose personal affections may have been already engaged, I have no fear of misconception on the part of right-minded readers, and shall not count as so much as the ghost of a flea the soul of the critic who concludes that I have quoted these passages in order to show how in my youth a great man praised me. I have quoted them because I believe they illustrate, as hardly anything else can, the sweetest and most intimate, if not the highest and noblest side of Rossetti's nature, that side, namely, which showed his capacity for the most disinterested friendship. And when I think of the traffic which too often goes by that name, the miserable commerce of give and take, the little-hearted barter in which self-love usually counts on being the gainer, I cannot but think that in letters like these, to an unknown beginner, Rossetti shows that with his other gifts he had the very genius of friendship itself.

Not to me only, as I now know, did he show sympathy and unselfishness, for the stories are not few or rare of how he gave his time and energies – and even in some cases sacrificed a little of his personal aims and ambitions – in order to forward the interests of his friends; but I think there was something exceptional in the friendship he gave to me. If he lived a solitary life in those days it was not because he might not have found society enough among importunate admirers round about him, who would have been only too eager to give him their company at the faintest hint or wink; but outside the narrow circle of intimate comrades he selected for his friend a young fellow in the country, half his age, who could bring him nothing but sympathy, and counted for so very little in a world in which he counted for so much.

I am not ashamed to say there are tears in my eyes and a lump in my throat when I read again, in Rossetti's letters, of the long evenings in his studio, when it was impossible for him to paint or draw by gaslight, and his loneliness was broken by writing to me; for I know that but for the unselfishness with which, in this way, he gave me so many hours of his silent company, and but for the encouragement, the strength and self-sacrifice he brought me, it would have taken me long to emerge from the commonplace round of daily life. Not that I was in any sense an object of pity, for I was no poor little drudge in a blacking warehouse, but, on the contrary, a much-indulged servant of an employer who had made me his friend; yet all the time I was a clerk in the lower middle-class of provincial life, and that is, perhaps, the wheel of life from which it is hardest to escape.

That I escaped from it at all was perhaps chiefly due to the generous extravagance with which Rossetti told me, in so many ways, that my "time could not be long delayed," and that in spite of my dark moods "all *must* come out well." There was not much to justify such bold predictions then, and when, years afterwards, on the publication of the first of my Manx novels, Rossetti's brother William said, "After all, Gabriel knew what he was doing." I was more moved by that than by many favourable articles; and since then, if I have spent countless precious hours reading the efforts of beginners and struggling to say good words of them, it has been only by way of balancing my reckoning with one who, in my early and dark days, did so much for me.

The correspondence from which I have quoted some pages went on without interruption for something more than a year, and during that time there was not, I suppose, a single day in which I did not either receive a letter from Rossetti or write to him. What my own letters were like I cannot any longer recall, nor is it necessary to remember; but Rossetti's letters, which were sometimes very long, being of six, eight, twelve, and even sixteen pages, constitute perhaps a larger body of writing than all his published compositions put together. It will, therefore, be a matter for no surprise that from that time forward, for several years to come, my life was my friendship with Rossetti.

I shall try in this book to tell the story of that

friendship, the greatest, the most intimate, the most beautiful that has ever come to me. In order to do so I must begin by giving an account of Rossetti's life before I knew him, and if this threatens to be a thrice told tale, I can at least promise that it will be brief.

CHAPTER III

THE STORY OF MY FRIEND'S LIFE

Dante Gabriel Rossetti (baptized Gabriel Charles Dante) was the elder son of Gabrielle Rossetti, a patriotic poet exiled from the Abruzzi, and of Frances Polidori, a daughter of Alfieri's secretary, and a sister of the young doctor who travelled with Lord Byron.

His father had taken part in the Neapolitan insurrection of 1820, and after the treachery of Ferdinand he was compelled to fly from his country. He arrived in England about 1823, married in the same year, was appointed Professor of Italian at King's College, and died in 1854.

Gabriel (the name by which his family always knew him) was born, as he had told me, on old May Day (the 12th) of 1828, in Charlotte Street, Portland Place. He had one brother, William Michael, and two sisters, Christina and Maria.

Gabrielle Rossetti's house was, as long as he lived, the constant resort of Italian refugees, from which I judge that though he did not live to see the returning glories of his country, he remained true to the last to the principles for which he had fought and suffered; but I do not gather that any of his children, least of all his elder son, felt any call of blood to participate

actively in the struggles of Italy. From the beginning
to the end Rossetti was, I think, an absolute Englishman.

The home of the Italian exile in London appears to
have been that of a poor scholar, and among the consequences of this condition was the inevitable one that
his children were brought up in an atmosphere of cul-
ture, and that his sons had to seek their own livelihood
as soon as possible. After a few years at King's College
School, Rossetti studied at the Royal Academy
Antique School; and he appears to have been a fairly
assiduous student. I remember that in later years,
when his habit of late rising was a stock subject of
banter between us, he told me with pride that at this
period he would rise at six in the morning once a week
to attend a life class, and breakfast on a buttered roll
and a cup of coffee at a stall at a street corner, so as not
to disturb the domestic arrangements by requiring the
servants to get up in the middle of the night.

So far as I can gather, he did not exercise the self-
denial very long, for he left the family roof after a few
years, and, in the interest of his studies, pitched his
tent with certain of his artist friends. These were Millais, Holman Hunt, Woolner, Deverell, Stephens, and,
above all, Madox Brown. With some of this group of
associates, while he was still under age, he started an
art movement, to which, half in jest, he gave the name
of Pre-Raphaelitism.

The group of young artists calling themselves Pre-
Raphaelites had begun to exhibit, to attract attention,
to excite discussion, and provoke censure, when Ruskin, already a great light in art criticism, came to the
rescue of the little brotherhood by writing a letter in

their defence in *The Times*, thus placing their movement in the category of serious efforts.

From early days Rossetti had written poetry, and it is clear from a letter already quoted that many of his most admired poems were the work of his first twenty-five years. Some of the best, showing marked originality of manner and substance, were obviously the product of his minority, and were accepted side by side by Pre-Raphaelitism in art as manifestations of Pre-Raphaelitism in literature. A magazine, called *The Germ*, was started to illustrate the new ideas, and later, in a kind of semi-affiliated way, came a kindred magazine, called *The Oxford and Cambridge*. Beyond, however, contributing a few of his poems to these periodicals, Rossetti made little or no attempt to publish his poetry, which, nevertheless, acquired a kind of subterranean reputation among his private friends.

His personal character in these days of early manhood is described as genial and generous, but also a little masterful. He was admittedly the king of his circle, and I fear it must be said that in all that constituted kingship he took care to rule. There appears to have been a certain determination of purpose which occasionally took the look of arbitrariness, sometimes even of selfishness, and a certain disregard of differing opinion which partook of tyranny.

Such is the picture given of Rossetti as a young man by some of those who knew him best; but there is another picture, equally authentic, which is, I think, a necessary counterpart. It is that of a robustious young fellow, of great intellectual pride perhaps, but of immense good-nature and irrsponsible spirits. Rossetti was never in any distinct sense a humorist, but there came to him at this period those outbursts of high spirits which act as safety-valves to serious natures. At such times he appears to have been utterly reckless, and to have plunged into any madcap escapade that might be afoot with complete heedlessness of consequences. Stories of misadventures, quips, and quiddities of every kind were then his delight, and he was by no means above the innocent ruffianism of the practical joke. To this period belong the tales of his rioting in those outrageous opinions on moral questions which appear to have shocked some staid people as the views of a young man in a Christian country in the middle of the nineteenth century; and to this period, too, belong the stories of tumultuous nights spent on the fringe of a wild Bohemia – manifestations of sheer intellectual vigour and animal spirits, not, I am sure, to be regarded in any more serious light.

But midway between the twenties and the thirties there came into his life an event that was to touch the deepest side of his nature. One day his friend Deverell, going with his mother into a milliner's shop in Oxford Street, saw through an open door a number of young girls at work in an inner room. Among the girls was one who had the most glorious mass of reddish-auburn hair, and as this was then the favourite Pre-Raphaelite colour, Deverell's interest was excited in a moment, and he whispered to his mother: "Ask that girl with the red hair if she will sit to me." After some hesitation, Mrs. Deverell did so; and on this chance hung the beginning of what is perhaps the most tragic series of incidents in modern literary life.

The girl sat as a model to Deverell, and through him to Rossetti, also. Her name was Elizabeth Eleanor Siddal, and she was the daughter of a singer at one of the dissenting chapels. Father and daughter had lately come from Sheffield, where certain records of them are still preserved. The girl was young and beautiful, clever also in various ways, and she presently revealed a very marked aptitude for art. She became known to all the young artists of the Rossetti circle, and Ruskin appears to have taken a peculiar interest in her. It is said that to enable her to liberate herself from the thraldom of her menial occupation, yet not to wound her pride, the great critic, who was rich, offered to buy all the pictures she could paint, on condition that she should become a pupil of Rossetti. There appears to have been no difficulty about this, for the painter's interest in his young model had speedily ripened into love. In due course Rossetti and Elizabeth Siddal became engaged.

The young girl must have been a very remarkable creature. her face, as Rossetti painted it, shows intellect and sensibility in a high degree, but also a certain tendency to sadness. People who remembered her, however, spoke of her as cheerful and bright if not vivacious in that springtime of her youth.

They seem to have been happy in those early days, painting together, reading together, and even writing together; for the girl developed under Rossetti's tuition not only a wonderful eye for colour and an astonishing power of composition, but also a real appreciation of the higher poetic literature, and a capacity for reproducing it. While he, too, as we may plainly see without other knowledge than the internal evidences of his work, produced some of the most pure and perfect of his poems under the impulse of her presence and the inspiration of his first great love.

Then came a separation, and it is not easy for me to say what it was due to – so conflicting were the stories of those who claimed to know. I have heard that, beautiful and brilliant as Elizabeth Siddal was, she was not (as is natural) in the conventional sense an educated woman; and that at her own suggestion and by Rossetti's help she went away to school. I have also heard that at a moment of some difference Ruskin again interposed, with certain delicate overtures, which enabled her to return for further study to her native place. At all events, she left London and was away for a considerable time.

Meantime Rossetti, giving up poetry on finding, as he says, that it "impeded attention to what constituted another aim and a livelihood into the bargain", devoted himself entirely to his painting. At twenty-eight he undertook with two or three other young painters, to cover with frescoes the walls of the Union Debating Hall at Oxford; and whilst engaged upon this task he made the acquaintance of a group of undergraduates with whose names his own name has ever since been associated – Burne-Jones, Swinburne, and William Morris, as well as one other who proved to be among the strongest, purest, and most lasting influences upon his life, the lady, herself a model at the beginning, who afterwards became his friend Morris's wife.

What effect these new friendships, any or all of them, may have had on the relation in which he still stood to Elizabeth Siddal it would perhaps be hard to say; but I think evidences are not wanting in the poems written about this period of a new and disturbing element – a painful and even tragic awakening, a sense of a great passion coming too late, and above all, of a struggle between love and duty which augured less than well for the happiness of the marriage that was to come.

But Elizabeth Siddal returned to London, and (perhaps by the intervention of Ruskin, to whom passion was little and duty was much) Rossetti and she were married. Friends who saw much of them in the earlier days of their married life spoke of their obvious happiness, and protested, in particular against evil rumours circulated later, that nothing could have been more marked than Rossetti's zealous attentions to his young wife. All the same, it is true that very soon her spirits drooped, her art was laid aside, and much of the cheerfulness of home was lost to both of them. Her health failed, she suffered from neuralgia, and began to be a victim of nervous ailments of other kinds.

To allay her sufferings she took laudanum, at first in small doses, but afterwards in excess. A child came, but it was still-born; and then her mood, already sad, appears to have deepened to one of settled melancholy. I remember to have heard Madox Brown say that she would sit for long hours, with her feet inside the fender, looking fixedly into the fire. It is easy to believe that to a man so impressionable as Rossetti, so dependent on cheerful surroundings, so liable to dark moods of his own, this must have been a condition which made home hard to bear. If he escaped from it as often as possible it is perhaps only natural, and it is no less natural if his absence was misunderstood. I express no opinion at present, but the facts appear to point that way.

They were living in rooms in Chatham Place, by the old Blackfriars Bridge, and one evening, about half-past six, having been invited to dine with friends at a hotel in Leicester Square, they got into a carriage to go. It had been a bad day for the young wife, and they had hardly reached the Strand when her nervousness became distressing to Rossetti, and he wished her to return. She was unwilling to do so, and they went on to their appointment; but it may be assumed that her condition did not improve, for at eight o'clock they were back at home.

Soon after that Rossetti left his wife preparing to retire for the night, and went out again, apparently to walk. What happened to her during the hours in which she was alone, what impulse led her to the act she committed, whether it was due to an innocent accident common to persons in her low condition, or to dark if delusive broodings such as I may have occasion to indicate later, it is not needful to say now. When he returned at half-past eleven o'clock he found his rooms full of a strong odour of laudanum. His wife was breathing stertorously and lying unconscious on the bed. He called a doctor, who saw at once, what was only too obvious, that the lady had taken an overdose of her accumstomed sleeping draught. Other doctors were summoned, and every effort was made to save the patient's life; but after lingering several hours without recovering consciousness for a moment – and therefore without offering a word of spoken explanation – towards seven o'clock in the morning she died.

Next day an inquest was held, at which Rossetti,

though stunned and stupefied, had to give the evidence which is summarised in the foregoing statement. There had been no reason why his wife should wilfully take her own life – quite the contrary – and when he had left her about nine o'clock she seemed more at ease. The verdict was "accidental death". The proceedings of the coroner's court were reported in a short paragraph in one only of the London papers (I have a copy of it), and there the poet's name was wrongly spelled.

This was in 1862, no more than two years after the marraige that had been waited for so long. The blow to Rossetti was a terrible one. It was some days before he seemed to realize fully the loss that had befallen him; but after that his grief knew no bounds, and it first expressed itself in a way that was full of the tragic grace and beauty of a great renunciation.

Many of his poems had been, as I have said, inspired by and addressed to his wife, and at her request he had copied them out, sometimes from memory, into a little book which she had given to him for this purpose. With this book in his hand, on the day of her funeral, he walked into the room where her body lay, and quite unmindful of the presence of others, he spoke to his dead wife as though she could hear, saying the poems it contained had been written to her and for her and she must take them with her to the grave. With these words, or words to the same effect, he placed the little volume in the coffin, by the side of his wife's face, and wrapped it round with her beautiful golden hair, and it was buried with her in Highgate Cemetery.

It was long before Rossetti recovered. Perhaps he

was never the same man again. At least the brilliant and perhaps rather noisy young fellow, fond of intellectual gymnastics, and full of a sort of animal spirits, was gone for good; and though after a time he recovered a certain hilarity, there does not seem to have been much real joy in it. Not long after his wife's death he removed from Blackfriars Bridge and made his home in the house already referred to – Queen's House, Cheyne Walk, Chelsea.

Before leaving his old quarters he destroyed many things associated with his life there, among them being a great body of letters, some very valuable, from men and women eminent in literature and art, Ruskin, Tennyson, and Browning. Perhaps with the same view of cutting himself off from everything that was likely to remind him of his great loss, he separated himself from many of his former friends. It was, of course, the last course he ought to have taken, whether in the interests of his mental or bodily health, and the consequences of his isolation came only too quickly and lasted only too long.

CHAPTER IV

ROSSETTI BEFORE I MET HIM

Insomnia, that curse of the literary and artistic temperament, had been hanging about Rossetti for years;
and now he began to try opiates. He took them in
sparing quantities after the death of his wife, for had
he not, in that fact alone, the most fearful cause to
avoid their use? But presently he heard of the then
newly-found drug – chloral, which was, of course,
accredited at the beginning with all the virtues and
none of the vices of other known narcotics. Here,
then, was the thing he wanted; this was the blessed
discovery that was to save him from days of weariness
and nights of misery. Eagerly he procured it, and took
it nightly in small doses of ten grains each; it gave him
pleasant and refreshing sleep. He made no conceal-
ment of his habit; like Coleridge under similar circumstances, he rather elected to talk of it. Not yet had he
learned the sad truth, too soon to force itself upon
him, hat this dreadful drug was an evil power with
which he was to fight, almost down to his dying day, a
single-handed and losing battle.

It was not, however, for some years after he began
to use it that chloral produced any sensible effects of
an injurious kind, and meantime he pursued his calling

as a painter, making a substantial living and, though he never exhibited, an unmistakable reputation. After a while he amused himself, also, in furnishing his big house in various and novel and beautiful styles, and in filling a big garden at the back with a veritable menagerie of birds and beasts. Life recovered a measure of interest for him in other directions also, if only as the shadowy ghost of the glad spirit of happier years; and Queen's House began to hum with the doings of friends old and new – Swinburne, Morris, Burne-Jones, for a short while Meredith, and, of course, his ever constant and devoted brother, William.

Thus seven years passed, and during that time Rossetti, who frequently immersed himself in the aims and achievements of his friends, and witnessed their rise to fame and honour, began to think with pain of the aspirations as a poet which he had himself renounced, and to cast backward glances at the book he had buried in his wife's coffin. That book contained the only perfect copy of his poems, other copies being either incomplete or unrevised; and it is hardly to be wondered at that he asked himself at length if it could not be regained. The impulse of grief or regret, or even remorse, that had prompted him to the act of renunciation had been satisfied, and for seven years he had denied himself the reward of his best poetic effort – was not his penance at an end? It was doing no good to the dead to leave hidden in the grave the most beautiful works he had been able to produce – was it not his duty to the living, to himself, and perhaps even to literature, to recover and publish them?

If, in the daily sight of the growing reputation of younger men, his friends and comrades of no better genius, Rossetti began to be influenced by thoughts like these, without reflecting that while it may have been an act of emotional weakness to bury his poems, it would be an act of desecration to take them up again, I set it down to the constant companionship at that period of a man of whom I shall have occasion to speak later on, a person out of another world altogether, a daring, reckless, unscrupulous soldier of fortune, very clever, very plausible, very persuasive, but totally destitute of delicate feeling, and almost without the moral sense.

Under this man's direction the exhumation, when Rossetti had brought himself to agree to it, was eventually carried out. According to his own account, given to me twelve years afterwards, the preparations were endless before the work could be done. But at length the licence of the Home Secretary was obtained, the faculty of the Consistory Court was granted, and one night, seven and a half years after the burial, a fire was built by the side of the grave of Rossettis' wife in Highgate Cemetery, the grave was opened, the coffin was raised to the surface, and the buried book was removed.

I remember that I was told, with much else which it is unnecessary to repeat, that the body was apparently quite perfect on coming to the light of the fire on the surface, and that when the book was lifted, there came away some of the beautiful golden hair in which Rossetti had entwined it.

While the painful work was being done the unhappy author of it, now keenly alive to its gravity, and already torturing himself with the thought of it as a deed of sacrilege, was sitting alone, anxious and full of self-reproaches, at the house of the friend who had charge of the exhumation, until, later than midnight, he returned to say it was all over.

The volume was not much worse for the years it had lain in the earth, but nevertheless it was found necessary to take it back to Rossetti, that illegible words might be deciphered and deficiencies filled in. This was done, with what result of fresh distress can easily be imagined; and then, with certain additions of subsequent sonnets, the manuscript was complete. Under the simple title of "Poems" it was published in 1870, fifteen to twenty years after the greater part of it was produced, and when the author was forty-two.

The success of the book was immediate and immense, six or seven considerable editions being called for in rapid succession. Appearing in the same season as Disraeli's "Lothair", it ran, from the bookseller's standpoint, a neck-and-neck race with a political romance which owed much of its popularity to recognizable portraiture of living persons. It was reviewed with enthusiasm on nearly every side, and it was at once the literary sensation and the social event of the hour.

It would perhaps be difficult to assign to any single cause this extraordinary success of a book whose popular qualities were obviously inconsiderable, whether, as Swinburne said in a noble essay full of splendid praise, to those innate qualities of beauty and strength which are always the first and last constituents of poetry that abides, or to the sudden explosion of the enthusiasm which had lived a subterranean life for so many years while the poems were in manuscript; or yet, as I think more probable, to the flick of interest and curiosity which came of a rumour of the book's romantic history, culminating in its burial for so many years in the grave of the woman whose love and beauty had inspired it.

Whatever the cause of the book's immediate success, there can be no doubt that Rossetti himself took great delight in it, and that in the first flush of his new-found happiness he began afresh with great vigour on poetic creation, producing one of the most remarkable ballads of his second volume within a short time of the publication of the first. But then came a blow which arrested his energies and contributed to bring his literary activities to a long pause.

About a year after the appearance of the "Poems", an article was published in one of the most influential of the reviews, the *Contemporary*, which was in general a denunciation of the sensual tendencies of the age, in art, music, poetry, and the drama, and, in particular, an impeachment of the poetry of Swinburne, William Morris, and especially of Rossetti, who were said to have "bound themselves into a solemn league and covenant to extol fleshliness as the distinct and supreme end of poetic and pictorial art, to aver that poetic expression is better than poetic thought, and, by inference, that the body is greater than the soul, and sound superior to sense".

The article, which was entitled "The Fleshly School of Poetry", a name that was in itself an offence, suggesting the shambles and wounding the very sensibilities which it was supposed to defend, was undoubtedly written with great vigour, much knowledge of literature, and an immense power of popular appeal. It produced a sensible effect, awakening that moral conscience which in the English people always slumbers, like the conventional lion, with one eye open, and being quickly followed by articles in the same spirit appearing in other reviews and newspapers of equal or yet greater standing.

On its publication in the *Contemporary* the article bore the signature "Thomas Maitland", but it afterwards became known that the actual writer was Robert Buchanan, then a young author who had risen to considerable distinction as a poet, and was consequently suspected, no doubt without injustice, of being actuated by feelings of envy rather than by desire for the public good.

It was an unpleasant controversy, but at this distance of time it would show ignorance of the literature of the period to deny that there were some grounds for Buchanan's attack. There was manifest in the poetry of certain English writers a tendency to deviate from wholesome reticence. This dangerous tendency came to us from France, where deep-seated unhealthy passion so gave shape to the glorification of gross forms of animalism as to excite alarm that what had begun with the hideousness of *Femmes Damnées* would not even end there. Finally, the unpleasant truth demanded to be spoken – by whomsoever had courage enough to utter it – that to deify mere lust was an offence and an outrage. So much for the justice on Buchanan's side. With the mistaken criticism linking the writers of Dante's time with French writers of the time of Baudelaire it is hardly necessary to deal. On the other hand, it must be said that the sum total of all the English poetry written in imitation of the worst forms of this French excess was probably less than one hundred lines. What was really reprehensible in the English imitation of the poetry of the French school was therefore, too inconsiderable to justify a wholesale charge against it of an endeavour to raise the banner of a black ambition whose only aim was to ruin society. Rossetti, who was made to bear the brunt of attack, was a man who never by direct avowal, or yet by inference, displayed the faintest conceivable sympathy with the French excesses in question, and never wrote a line that was consciously inspired by unwholesome passion.

That certain lines in Rossetti's love sonnets contained phrases that for the better part of two thousand years have been sacred to the highest mysteries of religion must not be denied, but this is only another proof that the deepest thing in him was the spirit of the old type of Italian Catholic. As for the poem "Jenny", which was the common ground of offence, it is, as Rossetti said to me later, nothing less than a sermon, unless, as I should myself prefer to say, much of it is like the Psalms or the Hebrew prophets, and not unworthy of either.

> Like a toad within a stone
> Seated while Time crumbles on;
> Which sits there since the earth was curs'd
> For Man's transgression at the first;
> Which, living through all centuries,
> Not once has seen the sun arise;
> Whose life, to its cold circle charmed,
> The earth's whole summers have not warmed;
> Which always – whitherso the stone
> Be flung – sits there, deaf, blind, alone –
> Aye, and shall not be driven out
> Till that which shuts him round about

Break at the very Master's stroke,
And the dust thereof vanish as smoke,
And the seed of Man vanish as dust:
Even so within this world is Lust.

If there is any purer or nobler writing than this in English poetry I have yet to find it.

To say that Rossetti felt the charges made against him is not to express his sense of them. He who had withheld his pictures from exhibition from dread of the distracting influences of public opinion; he who for fifteen years had kept back his poems from print in obedience first to an extreme modesty of personal estimate, and afterwards to the command of a mastering remorse, was of all men the one most likely to feel deeply and incurably the wicked slander, born in the first instance of jealousy, that he had unpacked his bosom of unhealthy passions and demoralised the public mind.

If what Rossetti did, under this first fire of the enemy, seems weak or futile, let it be said that only those who know by experience what it is to have this foul accusation made against them, can have any idea of its distracting power. In the first moments of his indignation, he wrote a full and point-by-point rejoinder, printed it as a pamphlet, had a great number struck off; then destroyed every copy. After that he wrote a temperate but not very effectual letter to *The Athenaeum*; but finding that the accusations he rebutted were repeated immediately with increasing bitterness, he lost hope of stemming the tide of unrelenting assault, and announced his intention of abandoning poetic composition.

One by one some of the remaining friends of earlier

years seemed now to have left him. Whether, as I later heard certain of them say, they wearied a little of Rossetti's absorption in the critical attacks made upon him – thinking he put them out of proportion, or interpreted their origin and intention by a light that was scarcely consistent with sanity – or whether Rossetti, on his part (as one of the letters I have quoted appears to show), began to think of his old comrades as "summer friends" who fell away at the first breath of winter, the result was the same – he shut himself up in his big house in yet more absolute seclusion than before.

Nor did the mischief end there. The chloral which he had first taken in small doses, he began now, in moments of physical prostration and nervous excitement, to indulge in to excess; and as a consequence he went through a series of terrible though intermittent illnesses, inducing a morbid condition, in which he was the victim of many painful delusions. Among them, as was perhaps natural, were some that related to the exhumation of his wife's body, and the curse that was supposed to have followed him for that desecration. This was an idea very liable to torment a mind so susceptible to supernatural suggestion as Rossetti's; and although one's soul cries out against a torture that was greater than any sins of his deserved, one cannot but welcome the thought that the seclusion to which he doomed himself, and the illness from which he suffered, were due to something more serious and more worthy of a man than the hostile article of a jealous fellow-poet.

Several years passed during which Rossetti lived in the closest retirement, seeing only the two or three friends who had been always with him, Madox Brown and his faithful and unfailing brother, William; and then light came and he began in the fuller sense to live again. Letters and articles reached him from many quarters, from foreign countries and distant colonies, showing that adverse criticism had not quenched the light of his book. New friends came, too, to take the place of those who had gone "from causes only too varying", and unquestionably the first of these – the first in the confidence reposed in him and the affection felt for him – was Theodore Watts-Dunton, known at that time as Walter Theodore Watts. Next to Watts, perhaps, among later friends came Frederic Shields, an artist from Manchester, whose power as a draughts-man and qualities as a man Rossetti held in high esteem. Others there were, too, such as Dr. Hake, himself a poet of some distinction, whose soothing friendship brought lasting solace; and finally, if I may say so, there was myself, coming into Rossetti's life under the conditions I have described.

I am older by twenty odd years at this time of writing than Rossetti was when I first knew him, and perhaps I can understand better now than I did then what interest I had for one who had twice my years. In default of the knowledge and the judgment that older friends could bring, and in spite of the difference of our education and gifts, I must have stood beside him like his youth, with its eagerness, its hopes, its dreams, its aspirations. This was just what was wanted at that period by the great man who had so lately come out of the shadowed valley, but was lonely enough yet, not-withstanding the frequent company of loyal com-rades, to find comfort and cheer in the sympathy of a young and enthusiastic stranger. He began to try his hand again at poetic composition, to send me some of his new poems, and to write of others with a freedom and familiarity that were entirely flattering.

"I am just finishing a ballad on the death of James I of Scotland. . . . It is a ripper, I can tell you, my boy."

It was clear that life was beginning to take a brighter outlook, and that he was preparing to publish again.

He was even thinking of exhibiting his pictures.

"I am painting a picture of modern life begun long ago, and when I finish it, *may* be showing some things one way or another. This also in thine ear."

"Your letter has crossed one of mine, but a solitary evening (rather exceptional with me now, as you will be glad to hear) leads to my writing again."

"Answer this when you can. I like getting your letters. The last was a goodly one."

"I hope sincerely that we may have further and closer opportunities of intercourse. . . . I should welcome your advent in London warmly."

Such, then, was Rossetti when I first knew him and during the earlier period of our correspondence, and now the time had come when I was to meet him face to face. There can be no necessity to describe the feelings with which I went forward to that first interview. Believing that my friend of nearly fifty years ago has entered into the company of the immortals, and that a century hence everything will be of interest that gets close to him at any period, my portrait may perhaps exceed in details, but it shall not fail in fidelity.

I cannot, of course, claim for my picture that it will represent Rossetti as he was from first to last, or yet as he appeared to older friends, who knew him through varying phases of his changeful career; but it shall at least be true to Rossetti as he appeared to me, twenty-five years his junior, and coming to him, full of admiration and affection, during the last years of his life.

CHAPTER V

MY FIRST MEETING WITH ROSSETTI

It was in 1880 that I saw Rossetti for the first time. Being somewhat reduced in health, I had contemplated a visit to one of the South Coast watering-places, and wrote saying that in passing through London I should like to avail myself of his oft-repeated invitation to visit him. By return of post came two letters, the one obviously written and posted within an hour or two of the other. In the first of these he said:

"I will be truly glad to meet you when you come to town. You will recognize the hole-and-cornerest of all existences; but I'll read you a ballad or two, and have Brown's report to back my certainty of liking you."

In the second letter he said:

"I would propose that you should dine with me on Monday at 8.30, and spend the evening. P.S. – Of course when I speak of your dining with me, I mean *tête-à-tête*, and without ceremony of any kind. I usually dine in my studio, and in my painting coat. D. G. R."

Cheyne Walk was unknown to me at the time of my first visit to Rossetti, except as the locality in which men and women eminent in literature were residing. It was not even then as picturesque as it appears to be in certain familiar engravings, for the embankment and the gardens that separated it from the main thorough-fare had already taken something from its quaint beauty; but it still possessed attractions which it has since lost, among them a look of age, which contrasted agreeably with the spick-and-span newness of neigh-bouring districts, and the slumbrous atmosphere as of a cathedral close, drowsing in the autumn sun to the murmur of the river which flowed in front, and the rustle of the trees that grew between.

Every foot of the old Walk was sacred ground to me then, for George Eliot, after her marriage with Mr. Cross, had lately come to, I think, No. 5; while at No. 5, in the second street to the westward Carlyle was still living, and a little beyond Cheyne Row stood the modest cottage wherein Turner died. Rossetti's house was No. 16, and I found it answering in external appearance to the frank description he had given of it. It seemed to be the oldest house in the Walk, and the exceptional size of its gate piers and the height and weight of its gate and railings suggested to me, as an architect, that perhaps at some period it had stood alone, commanding as grounds a large part of the space occupied by the houses on either side.

The house itself was a plain Queen Anne erection, much mutilated by the introduction of unsightly bow windows, the brick work falling into decay, the paint in need of renewal, the windows dull with the dust of months, the sills bearing more than the suspicion of cobwebs, the angles of the steps to the porch and the untrodden flags of the little court leading up to them overgrown with moss and weed, while round the walls and up the reveals of door and windows were creeping the tangled branches of the wildest ivy that ever grew untouched by shears.

Such was the exterior of the house of the poet-painter when I walked up to it on the autumn evening of my earliest visit. The interior of the house, when with a trembling heart I first stepped over the threshold, seemed to be at once like and unlike the outside. The hall had a puzzling look of equal nobility and shabbiness, for the floor was paved with white marble, which was partly covered by a strip of worn out coconut matting. Three doors led out of the hall, one at each side and one in front, and two corridors opened into it, but there was no sign of a staircase; neither was there any daylight, except the little that was borrowed from a fanlight which looked into the porch.

I took note of these things in the few minutes I stood waiting in the hall, and if I had to sum up my first impressions of the home of Rossetti, I should say it looked like a house that no woman had ever dwelt in – a house inhabited by a man who had once felt a vivid interest in life, but was now living from day to day.

Very soon Rossetti came to me through the doorway in front, which proved to be the entrance to his studio. Holding out both hands and crying "Hulloa!" he gave me that cheery, hearty greeting which I came to recognize as belonging to him alone, perhaps, of all the men I have ever known.

Leading the way into the studio, he introduced me to his brother William, who was there on one of the evening visits which at intervals of a week he made then with unfailing regularity.

I should have described Rossetti, at that time, as a

man who looked quite ten years older than his actual age (fifty-two); of full middle height, and inclining to corpulence; with a round face that ought, one thought, to be ruddy, but was pale; with large grey eyes, that had a steady, introspective look, and were surmounted by broad, protrusive brows, and divided by a clearly pencilled ridge over the nose, which was well cut, and had breathing nostrils resembling the nostrils of a high-bred horse.

His mouth and chin were hidden beneath a heavy moustache and an abundant beard, which had once been mixed black-brown and auburn, but were now thickly streaked with grey. His forehead was large, round, without protuberances, and very gently receding to where thin black curls began to roll round to the ears. I though his head and face singularly noble, and from the eyes upward full of beauty.

His dress was not conspicuous, being rather negligent than eccentric, and only remarkable for a straight sack-coat (his "painting coat") buttoned close to the throat, descending at least to the knees, and having large perpendicular pockets, in which he kept his hands almost constantly while he walked to and fro. His voice, even in the preliminary courtesies of conversation, was, I thought, the richest I had ever heard. It was a deep, full baritone, with easy modulations and undertones of infinite softness and sweetness, yet capable, as I speedily found, of almost illimitable compass, having every gradation of tone at command for the recitation or reading of poetry.

Such was Rossetti as he seemed to me when I saw him first – a noticeable man, indeed; an Englishman in his stolid build, an Italian in the dark fire of his face, a man of genius in the strength and individuality which expressed themselves in his outer personality without singularity or affectation.

The studio was a large, irregular room, measuring, perhaps, thirty feet by twenty, and structurally puzzling to one who saw it for the first time. The fireplace was at one end of the room, and at either side of it hung a number of drawings in chalk, chiefly studies of female heads, all very beautiful, and all by Rossetti himself. Easels of various size, some very large, bearing partly-painted pictures in different stages of progress, stood at irregular angles nearly all over the floor, leaving room only for a few pieces of furniture. There were a large sofa, under a holland cover, somewhat baggy and soiled, two low easy chairs similarly apparelled (now in my own study at Greeba) a large bookcase with a glass front surmounted by a yellow copy of the Stratford bust of Shakespeare – also now in my home. Two carved cabinets, and a little writing-desk and cane-bottomed chair were in the corner, near a small window, which was heavily darkened by the thick foliage of the trees that grew in the garden beyond.

As I had arrived late, and the light was failing, Rossetti immediately drew up an easel containing a picture he wished me to see, and I recall a large canvas full of the bright sunshine of spring, with a beautfiul lady sitting reading in a tree that was heavily laden with pink and white blossom. Remembering the sense of the open air which the picture conveyed, I cannot forget the pallid face of the painter as he stood beside it, or the close atmosphere of his studio, with its smell of paint and the musty odour of accumulated treasures

44

lying long undisturbed in a room that can have been rarely visited by the winds of heaven.

I helped Rossetti to push the big easel out of the way, and then he dropped down on the sofa at full length, letting his head lie low on the cushion, and throwing his feet up on the back. In this attitude, which I afterwards saw was a favourite one with him, he began the conversation by telling me, with various humorous touches, how like I was to what a well-known friend of his (Burne-Jones) had been at my age; and then he bantered me for several minutes on what he called my "robustious" appearance, compared with that which he had been led to expect from gloomy reports of uncertain health.

It was all done in the easiest conceivable way, and was so playful and so natural, as coming from a great and famous man on his first meeting with a young fellow half his age, who regarded him with a reverence only modified by affection, that it might fairly have conveyed any impression on earth save the right one, that Rossetti was a bungle of nerves, a creature of emotions all compact, and that, at this period, a visit from a new friend, however harmless and insignificant, was an ordeal of almost tragic gravity to him.

Then, one by one, he glanced at certain of the more personal topics that had arisen in the course of our correspondence, and I soon saw that he was a ready, fluent, and graceful talker, with an unusual incisiveness of speech which gave the effect of wit, even when it was not wit. I was struck with a trick he had of snapping his long finger-nails as he talked, and the constant presence of his hands, which were small and smooth and delicate as a young girl's, with tapering fingers, that he seemed to be always looking at and playing with.

Very soon the talk became general, his brother William, who had hitherto been silent, joining in at intervals; and then Rossetti spoke without appearance of reserve of the few intimate friends who frequented his house at that period, telling me, among other things, that Watts (afterwards Watts-Dunton) had a head like Napoleon's, "whom he detests", he said with a chuckle; that Frederic Shields was as hysterical as Shelley, and Ford Madox Brown, whom I had met, as sententious as Dr. Johnson.

I thought Rossetti was amusing himself by bantering his friends in their absence, in the assured confidence that he was doing so in the presence of a well-wisher; but it was interesting to observe that after any particularly lively sally or dash of personal ridicule, he would pause in the midst of his laughter, which was a deep, full-chested roar, to say something in a sober tone that was intended to convey the idea that he had really said nothing at all.

We dined in a little green dining-room, surrounded by round mirrors and entered from the left of the hall, and I remember that as we dined, Rossetti, who seemed to be in the best of spirits, rattled off one or two of the rhymes, now called "Limericks", at the making of which nobody who ever attempted that form of amusement has been known to match him. He could turn them out as fast as he could talk, with such point, such humour, such building-up to a climax, that even when they verged on the personal, or yet the profane (as I fear they sometimes did), it was impossible to receive the last word without a shout. I recall that on this occasion he recited for my amusement a rhyme he had made on a poet friend who had lost his hair; and with the sting of it still in my mind, I should not wonder if the almost fatal facility he had in the writing of satirical doggerel sometimes cost the poet dear.

Dinner over, we went back to the studio, and then I asked Rossetti to fulfil his promise to read some of his new ballads to me. He responded readily, like a man who was glad to read his poetry to an admirer, only apologizing to his brother, who had heard everything before, but cheerfully consented to listen again.

Unlocking a section of the big bookcase, and again unlocking an old carved box that stood on one of the shelves (he left it to me later), he took out a small manuscript volume, and after putting on a second pair of spectacles over the pair he usually wore, he read "The White Ship".

It seemed to me that I had never heard anything at all equal to Rossetti's elocution, if reading so entirely without conscious art can be called by that name. The poet's deep rich voice lent music to the music of the verse; it rose and fell in the passages descriptive of the wreck with something of the surge and sibilation of the sea itself; in the tender passages it was as soft and low as a girl's; and in the pathetic stanzas at the close it was indescribably moving.

The evening had gone by the time the ballad was ended, and when William Rossetti rose to go I got up to go with him. Then it was arranged that on returning through London after my holiday on the South Coast I should dine with Rossetti again, and sleep the night at his house. He came into the hall to see us off, and down to the last his high spirits never failed him. I recall some further bantering as I was going out at the door, and the full-chested laugh that followed us over the little paved court between the house and the gate.

Our little night journey, William's and mine, in the hansom cab which was to drop me at the door of the "hole-and-cornerest" of all hotels, which, as a young countryman ignorant of London, I somehow ferreted out, is made ever memorable to me by a dazed sense I had of having seen and spoken to and spent an evening with what I thought one of the gods of the earth. That is a delicious sensation that only comes once perhaps to any of us, and then in our youth; and it was after my first meeting with Rossetti that it came to me.

CHAPTER VI

A NIGHT AT CHEYNE WALK

About a fortnight later I returned to Cheyne Walk and was welcomed with the same cheery "Hulloa" from Rossetti, who was lying, as I entered the studio in the early evening, in his favourite attitude on the couch. He was alone on this occasion, and, notwithstanding the warmth of my reception, I noticed that he was in some respects a changed man, his spirits being lower, his face more weary, even his voice more tired.

I remember that, in answer to inquiries as to where I had been and what I had been doing, I talked with the animation of a young man interested in life in many aspects; of the delightful Halliwell-Phillipps (with whom I had been staying at Brighton) and his group of good old Shakespearean dry-as-dusts, and then of Henry Irving, who was rising into celebrity as a Shakespearean actor. Rossetti lay on the sofa and listened, dropping out occasional observations, such as that Miss Herbert, an actress and a former friend, had spoken long ago of a young fellow in her company named Irving, predicting great success for him.

But it was soon made clear to me that the poet was more amused by the impetuous rush as of fresh air from the outer world, which came to him with my company, than interested in the affairs of the outer world itself. Indeed, I speedily saw that Rossetti knew very little of what was going on outside the close atmosphere of his own house and the circle of his literary and artistic activities, and that he did not care to know.

Expecting my return, he had pulled out a huge canvas into a position in which it could be seen, and it was then I saw for the first time the painter's most important picture, "Dante's Dream". The effect produced upon me by that wonderful work, so simple in its composition, yet so noble in its feeling and so profound in its emotion, has probably been repeated a thousand times since in minds more capable of appreciating the technical qualities of the painter's art; but few or none can know what added power of appeal the great picture had as I saw it then, under the waning light of an autumn afternoon, in the painter's studio, so full of the atmosphere of the picture itself, and with the painter beside it, so clearly a man out of another age.

Rossetti told me something of the history of "Dante's Dream", how it had been commissioned by a friend and returned in exchange for a replica because of its great size, which made it practically impossible to a private collection. Standing before the "Dante" we talked of the art of painting, and I recall, with some amusement, the light way in which the author of this product of genius spoke of the gifts that had gone to produce it.

"Does your work take much out of you in physical energy?" I asked.

"Not my painting, certainly," said Rossetti,

"though in earlier years it tormented me more than enough. Now I paint by a set of unwritten but clearly defined rules, which I could teach to any man as systematically as you could teach arithmetic."

"Still," I said, "there's a good deal in a picture like this beside what you can do by rule – eh?"

I laughed, he laughed, and then he said, as nearly as I can remember:

"Conception, no doubt; but beyond that, not much. Painting, after all, is the craft of a superior carpenter. The part of a picture that is not mechanical is often trivial enough."

And then, with the suspicion of a twinkle in his eye, he said:

"I shouldn't wonder now if you imagine that one comes down here in a fine frenzy every morning to daub canvas."

More laughter on both sides, and then I said I certainly imagined that a supeior carpenter would find it hard to paint another "Dante's Dream", which I considered the best example I had yet seen of the English school.

"Friendly nonsense," replied my frank host; "there is now no English school whatever."

"Well," I said, "if you deny the name to others who lay more claim to it, will you not at least allow it to the three or four painters who started with you in life – the Pre-Raphaelites, you know."

"Not at all, unless it is to Brown, and he's more French than English. Hunt and Jones have no more claim to it than I have. Pre-Raphaelites! A group of young fellows who couldn't draw!"

With this came one of his full-chested laughs, and

then quickly behind it:

"As for all the prattle about Pre-Raphaelitism, I confess to you I am weary of it, and long have been. Why should we go on talking about the visionary vanities of half-a-dozen boys? We've all grown out of them, I hope, by now."

We dined in the studio that night, and I recall the suggestion of my host's Italian origin in the thick pipes of macaroni cooked dry and then smothered in thick layers of cheese, and the red Chianti, diluted with water; but there was no sweet or coffee, and Rossetti did not smoke.

Returning after dinner to my inquiry as to whether his work took much out of him, he replied that his poetry usually did.

"In that respect," he said, "I am the reverse of Swinburne. For his method of production inspiration is indeed the word. With me the case is different. I lie on the couch, the racked and tortured medium, never permitted an instant's relief until the thing in hand is finished."

Then, at my request, taking the same little manuscript volume from the small oak box in the locked section of the bookcase, he read his unpublished ballad, "Rose Mary", telling me it had been written in the country shortly after the publication of his first volume of poems, that it had occupied only three weeks in the writing, and that the physical prostration ensuing had been more than he would care to go through again.

He then read to me a great body of the new sonnets, which, in his forthcoming volume, he intended to incorporate in a section to be called "The House of

Life". Sitting in that studio listening to the rise and fall of his wonderful voice, and looking up at the chalk drawings that hung on the walls, I realized how truly he had said in correspondence, that the feeling pervading his pictures was such as his poetry ought to suggest. The affinity between the two seemed to me at that moment to be the closest and most complete – the same half-sad, half-resigned view of life, the same glimmerings of uncertain hope, the same foreshadowings of despair.

Once or twice after the emotion of the written words had broken up his voice, he would pause and laugh a little (a constrained laugh in his throat), and say:

"I dare say you think it odd to hear an old fellow read such love poetry, as much of this is, but I may tell you that the larger part of it was written when I was as young as you are."

I remember that he read with especial emotion, and in a voice that could barely support itself, the pathetic sonnet entitled "Without Her":

> "What of her glass without her?
> ... Her pillowed place
> Without her? ...
> What of the heart without her? ..."

These lines came with tears of voice, subsiding at length into something like a suppressed sob, and they were followed by an interval of silence. But after a moment, as if trying to explain away his emotion and to deprive it of any personal reference in my mind, he said:

"All poetry affects me deeply, and often to tears. It

doesn't need to be pathetic or yet tender to produce this result."

Then he went on to say that he had known in his life two men, and two only, who were similarly sensitive – Tennyson and his friend Bell Scott.

"I once heard Tennyson read 'Maud'," he said, "and while the fiery passages were given with a voice and vehemence which he alone could compass, the softer passages and the songs made the tears run down his cheeks like rain. Morris is a fine reader too; and so of his kind, although a little prone to sing-song, is Swinburne. Browning both reads and talks well, at least he did so when I knew him intimately as a young man."

I asked if he had ever heard Ruskin read, and he replied:

"I must have done so, but I remember nothing clearly. On one occasion, however, I heard him deliver a speech, and that was something never to forget. When we were young we helped Frederick Denison Maurice by taking classes at his Working Men's College, and there Charles Kingsley and others made speeches and delivered lectures. Ruskin was asked to do something of the kind, and at length consented. He made no sort of preparation for the occasion; I knew he did not – we were together at his father's house the whole of the day. At night we drove down to the College, and then he made the most wonderful speech I had ever heard. I doubted at the time if any written words of his were equal to it – such flaming diction, such emphasis, such appeal! Yet he had written his first and second volumes of 'Modern Painters' by that time."

Here I cannot resist the temptation to interrupt the story of my second visit to Rossetti's house by saying how far I found Rossetti's picture of Ruskin in his early manhood agreed with my own knowledge of him at that time and later. I had already made Ruskin's acquaintance by correspondence in connection with the literary society I had founded at Liverpool. I never knew him intimately, but he had written to me a not inconsiderable number of short letters at that shadowed period of his life. I have never attempted to publish these letters, and it is unlikely that I shall ever do so. They fully bear out Rossetti's description of Ruskin's speech in its flaming diction, and its emphasis, but they also bear marks of the excess which came to his brilliant intellect with a temporary disorder. But in the last year but one before Ruskin's death, I had the pleasure to meet him in the flesh in his house at Coniston. He had then been for years silent, and so far as active interest in the affairs of life went, he had long been dead. I found him very old and bent and feeble, a smaller, frailer man than I looked for; well in health both of body and mind, but with faculties that were dying down very slowly and gently, and almost imperceptibly – as the lamp dies down when the oil fails in it.

His head was not so full as I expected to find it, and it hardly seemed to me in form or size either grand or massive; his eyes were slow and peaceful, having lost their former fire; and his face, from which the quiet life of later years had smoothed away the lines of strong thought and torturing experience, was too much hidden by a full grey beard. He spoke very little, and always in a soft and gentle voice that might have been the voice of a woman; but he listened to everything and smiled frequently. All the fiery heat of earlier days was gone, all the nervous force of the fever patient, all the capacity for noble anger and righteous wrath. Nothing was left but gentleness, sweetness, and quiet courtesy – the unruffled peace of a breathless evening that is gliding into a silent night. In short, his whole personality left the impression of the approach of death; but death so slow, so gradual, so tender and so beautiful, that it almost made one in love with it to see it robbed of every terror.

I think he was glad to see me for the sake of what I could tell him of certain friends of his early manhood, from whom the world had long divided him; and perhaps because, as he said, I resembled one of them as he had known him thirty years before. So he sat up until nearly eleven o'clock on the two nights of my visit (his usual hour being nine), and in default of his own talking, which I should have dearly loved to listen to if the days had not gone by for that eloquent tongue to speak freely, I talked of some of the men and things he loved to hear about – Shields, Burne-Jones and Rossetti.

On the morning of my departure I went up to Ruskin's bedroom to say good-bye to him. It was a small chamber of, perhaps, twelve feet by twelve, covered from ceiling to floor with water-colour pictures by Turner, which made the air warm with their glow and splendour. The windows of the little room looked out on a far different scene from the scenes pictured within. It was winter time. Coniston Old Man was heavily capped with snow, and between the house and the mountain there were the half-frozen lake and the floating mists of the moorland. And standing there, in the midst of those priceless treasures, with the fiery soul beside me now tempered with age and softened by the joys of home and the love of devoted kindred, it was difficult to recall without emotion the moving passage which begins: "Morning dawns as I write – would that somebody had told me then –".

I was at Brantwood again the other day. Everything was the same, yet everything was different. The great spirit was gone.

CHEYNE WALK (CONTINUED)

Returning from this scarcely pardonable sin of digression to the story of my second visit to Rossetti – we sat up until four in the morning, no unaccustomed hour for him, as I afterwards learned, for he had never at any period been an early riser, and was then more than ever prone to reverse the natural order of sleeping and waking hours.

"I lie as long, or, say, as late, as Doctor Johnson used to," he said. "You shall never know until you discover it for yourself at what hour I rise."

And now I do not feel that I can omit to mention that just as we were getting up to go to bed, Rossetti revealed a new side of his character, or, more properly, a new phase of his mind, which gave me infinite anxiety and distress. Branching off at that late hour from an entirely foreign topic, he begged me to tell him the facts of an unlucky debate in which I had long before been engaged on a public platform with someone who had attacked him. He had read a short report of what had passed at a time when both my name and the name of his assailant were unknown to him, and now he wished to hear everything. I tried to avoid a circumstantial statement, being forewarned by his brother, on that night ride after my first visit, of the poet's peculiar sensitiveness to criticism; but Rossetti was "of imagination all compact", and my obvious desire to shelve the subject was plainly suggesting to his mind a thousand inferences that were infinitely more damaging than the fact. To avoid this result, I told him all, and there was not much to tell.

The lecture of mine on his poetry, which led to the beginning of our friendship, had been presided over on the platform at Liverpool by a public man of more than local celebrity. At the close of my passionate panegyric, in which I had, perhaps, dwelt too insistently on the spiritual influences animating the poet's work, my chairman rose, and, as nearly as I can remember, said:

"We have all listened with interest and admiration to the eloquent" (etc.), "but it would be wrong of me not to warn the audience against the teaching of the lecturer. So far from Rossetti being animated mainly, or even largely, by spiritual passion, he is the most sensuous, not to say sensual, of English poets, and in his character as artist I can best describe him as the greatest *animal* painter alive."

This, and a few similar strictures, partly provoked, it may be, by the misdirection of my own eulogy, followed by a heated reply from myself, rapturously applauded by an audience which was probably indifferent to the question in dispute and interested only in the unusual spectacle of a stand-up fight between the young lecturer and the city father, with a word or two of brusque characterization aimed at "Jenny", whom I had perhaps dwelt upon as a soiled Madonna, was all there was to repeat in the way of attack.

Rossetti listened but too eagerly to my narrative, with drooped head and changing colour, and then in a voice slower, softer, and more charged perhaps with emotion than I had heard before, said it was the old story, which began ten years earlier, and would go on until he had been hunted and hounded into his grave.

Startled, and indeed appalled, by so grave a view of what seemed to me after all an unimportant incident, and no more than an error of critical judgment, coupled with some intemperance of condemnation, for which my own heat had been partly to blame, I prayed of him to think no more of the matter, reproached myself with having yielded to his importunity, and begged him to remember that if one man held the opinions I had repeated, many men held contrary ones.

"It was right of you to tell me when I asked you," he said, "though my friends usually keep such facts from my knowledge. As to 'Jenny,' it is a sermon, nothing less. As I say, it is a sermon, and on a great world, to most men unknown, though few consider themselves ignorant of it. But of this conspiracy to persecute me – what remains to say, except that it is widespread and remorseless. One cannot but feel it."

I assured him that there existed no conspiracy to persecute him; that he had ardent upholders everywhere, though it was true that few men had found crueller critics. He shook his head, and said I knew that what he had alleged was true: namely, that an organized conspiracy existed, having for its object to annoy and injure him, and to hold him up to the public execration as an evil influence on his time. So tyrannical, he said, had the conspiracy become, that it

had altered the habits of his life, and practically confined him for years to the limits of his own home.

Growing impatient of this delusion, so tenaciously
held to against all show of reason, I forgot the disparity of our ages, and told him that what he was saying was no more than the fever of a morbid brain,
brought about by his reclusive habits of life, by shun-
ning intercourse with all the world save some half-
dozen or more intimate friends.

"You tell me," I said, "that you have rarely been
outside these walls for years; meanwhile your brain
has been breeding a host of hallucinations that are like
cobwebs in a dark corner. You have only to go out
again, and the fresh air will blow these things away."

He smiled – perhaps at the boldness of youth – a sad
smile, and then went on again for some moments
longer in the same strain. He came to closer quarters,
and distressed me by naming as enemies two public
men, one of them the outstanding statesman of the
time (who had lately given a pension to the critic who
had most savagely abused him), and three or four
authors of high repute, who had been his close friends
in earlier life, but had fallen away from him in later
years, owing to circumstances that had no relation to
alienated regard.

"You're all wrong," I said. "I'm sure you're all
wrong."

"Ah, well, let's go to bed," said Rossetti; and I
could see that his conviction was unshaken, and his
delusions (if such they were) remained.

We took candles from a table in the hall and went
up a narrow and tortuous staircase, which was otherwise dark, to a landing from which many rooms

seemed to open, so large was the house in which Rossetti lived alone, except for a cook and two maid-servants.

"You are to sleep in Watts's room tonight," he said, and then he suggested that before going to my own bedroom I should take a look at his. I cheerfully assented, but walking through the long corridor that led to the poet's room, we had to pass another apartment, and after a moment's pause, Rossetti opened the door and we went in. It was the drawing-room, a very large chamber, barely illuminated by the candles in our hands, and full of the musty odour of a place long shut up.

Suspended from the middle of the ceiling there hung a huge Venetian candelabra, from whose facets the candlelight glittered. On the walls were a number of small water-colour drawings in plain oak frames. Rossetti drew me up to the pictures, and I remember that they seemed to me rather crude in colour and in drawing, but very touching in sentiment (one in particular, representing a young girl parting from her lover on the threshold of a convent, being deeply charged with feeling), and that I said:

"I should have thought that the man who painted these pictures was rather a poet than a painter – who was it?"

Rossetti, who was standing before the drawing, as I see him still, in the dark room, with the candle in his hand, said in a low voice: "It was my wife. She had great genius."

His own bedroom was entered from another and smaller room, which he told me he used as a breakfast-room. The outer room was made fairly bright by another glittering chandelier (the property at one time, he said, of David Garrick). By the rustle of the trees against the window-pane, one realized that it over-looked the garden. But the inner room was dark with heavy hangings around the walls as well as about the bed (a black four-poster) and thick velvet curtains before the windows, so that the candles we carried seemed unable to light it, and our voices to sound muffled and thick.

An enormous black oak chimney-piece of curious design, having an ivory crucifix on the largest of its ledges, covered a part of one side of the room, and reached to the ceiling. Cabinets, a hip-bath, and the usual furniture of a bedroom occupied places about the floor, and in the middle of it, before a little couch, there was a small table on which stood a wired lantern containing a candle, which Rossetti lit from the open one in his hand, another candle lying by its side. I re-marked that he probably burnt a light all night, and he said that was so.

"My curse is insomnia," he added. "Two or three hours hence I shall get up and lie on the couch and, to pass away a weary hour, read this book" – a volume of Boswell's "Johnson" which he had taken out of the bookcase as we left the studio.

The I saw that on the table were two small bottles, sealed and labelled, and beside them was a little mea-suring glass. Without looking further, but with a pain-ful suspicion coming over me, I asked if that was his medicine.

"They say there's a skeleton in every cupboard," he said in a low voice. "That's mine; it's chloral."

When I reached the room I was to occupy for the

rest of the night, I found it, like Rossetti's bedroom, heavy with hangings, and black with antique picture panels; having a ceiling so high as to be out of all reach and sight, and being so dark from various causes that the candle seemed only to glitter in it.

Presently, Rossetti, who had left me in my room, came back, for no purpose that I can remember, except to say that he had much enjoyed my visit. I replied that I should never forget it.

"If you desire to settle in London," he said, "I trust you'll come and live with me, and then many such evenings must remove the memory of this one."

I laughed, for what he so generously hinted at seemed to me the remotest contingency.

"I have just taken sixty grains of chloral," he said as he was going out. "In four hours I shall take sixty more, and in four hours after that yet another sixty."

"Doesn't the dose increase with you?" I asked.

"It has not done so perceptibly in recent years. I judge I've taken more chloral than any man whatever. Marshall" (his medical man) "says if I were put into a Turkish bath I should sweat it at every pore."

As he said this, standing half outside the threshold, there was something in his tone and laugh suggesting that he was even proud of the accomplishment. To me it was a frightful revelation, accounting largely, if not entirely, for what had puzzled and distressed me in the delusions I have referred to.

And so, after four in the morning, amid the odour of bygone ages, with thoughts of that big and almost empty house, of the three women servants somewhere out of all reach and sound, of Rossetti in his muffled room, of that wired lantern, and the two bottles of chloral, I fell asleep.

When I awoke in the morning the white daylight was coming into my dark bedroom through the chinks of the closed shutters, which, being opened, disclosed a garden so large and so completely encompassed by trees as to hide almost entirely the surrounding houses. Remembering what I had heard of a menagerie of wild birds and tame beasts which Rossetti used to keep in this garden, I went down before breakfast to look at it.

The garden was of a piece with what I had seen of the house. A beautiful avenue of lime-trees opened into a grass plot of nearly an acre in extent. The trees were just as nature made them, and so was the grass, which was lying, in its broad blades, long, and dry, and withered, in ugly tufts, with weeds creeping up in the damp places, and moss growing on the gravel of the path. The wild birds and tame beasts were gone, but the sparrows were chirping from the trees in the sunshine of the clear Autumn morning, and one little linnet was singing from a bough of the chestnut that looked in at the window of Rossetti's bedroom, still blind with its closed shutters, though the hour was now late.

A pathway ran near to the wall round the four sides of the garden, and here, as I had heard the night before, Rossetti took his only fresh air and exercise, walking six times about the enclosure every day. So quiet, indeed so dead, was the overgrown place that it was difficult to believe it was in the heart of London; and looking up at the shuttered window, it was easy to wish it were not.

But if the back of the house was silent, the front of it

was full enough of life. I breakfasted alone in the little green dining-room, the room of the round mirrors, and it was flooded with sunshine, and even deafened with noise – the rattle of tradesmen's carts and the whoop of the butcher as he was scudding down the Walk.

Before leaving the house I went into the studio again to take another look at the great "Dante", and the silent place, with its faint odour of paint, its canvasses, full of glorious colour, its chalk drawings, in black and red, of women with beautiful but melancholy faces, seemed to sweep one back again in a moment to some Italian city of three centuries ago.

When I was about to leave the house at a late hour that morning Rossetti was not yet stirring, but his housekeeper (who was also his cook), an elderly body, nervous and anxious, and obviously perplexed by the conditions of her life in that strange house with a master of exceptional habits, came to me with a letter which, I think, she said she had found lying on the table in the outer room where Rossetti took his breakfast. It was a parting message from the poet, probably written in that interval of wakefulness in the middle of the night, when, as he had told me, he got up and read on the couch.

MY DEAR CAINE,

I forgot to say, Don't, please, spread details as to the story of 'Rose Mary.' I don't want it to be stale, or to get forestalled in the travelling of report from mouth to mouth. I hope it won't be too long before you visit town again – I will not for an instant question that you will then visit me also.

D. G. R.

I do not think anybody who has realized (as, indeed, should be most easy) the space that divided me – a young fellow, untried and unknown – from this great and illustrious man will wonder that he was absolutely irresistible to me; but if I have to formulate the emotions which possessed me as I left his house on the occasion of this second visit, I will say that it was not so much his genius as his unhappiness that held me as by a spell.

Before this, I had been attracted by admiration of his great gifts, but now I was drawn to him by something very nearly akin to pity for his isolation and suffering. Not that at this time he made demand of much compassion. Health was apparently whole with him, his spirits were good, and his energies were at their best. He had not yet known the full bitterness of the shadowed valley; not yet learned what it was to hunger for any cheerful society that would relieve him of the burden of the flesh. All that came later; and, meantime, Rossetti was to me the most fascinating, the most inspiring, the most affectionate, and the most magnetic of men.

Next morning I was at work with my drawing-board and T-square in the little office overlooking the builder's yard, busy with its workmen and carts and the commonplace traffic of modern life.

CHAPTER VIII

I BECOME ROSSETTI'S HOUSEMATE

I think the better part of a year passed before I saw Rossetti again; but meantime I was in constant correspondence with him, so that the continuity of our intercourse was never broken for so much as a day. Long afterwards, when he was very ill, he said to me:

"How well I remember the beginning of our correspondence, and how little did I think it would lead to such relations between us as have ensued! I was at that time very solitary and depressed from various causes, and the letters of a well-wisher, so young and so ardent, though unknown to me personally, brought a good deal of comfort."

"Your letters," I said, "were very valuable to me."

"Mine to you," he answered, "were among the largest body of literary letters I ever wrote, others being often letters on personal subjects."

"And so admirable in themselves," I added, "that many of them would bear to be printed exactly as you penned them."

"That," he said, "will be for you some day to decide."

Later still, I remember, at a very solemn moment he said:

"Caine, how long have we been friends?"

I replied: "Between three and four years."

"And how long did we correspond?"

"Three years, nearly."

"What numbers of my letters you must have! They may perhaps even yet be useful to you; otherwise our friendship may prove to have been more burden than service."

Only that I knew how unselfish had been the impulse which prompted the last remark, I might, perhaps, from that moment have regarded the publication of Rossetti's letters to me as a sort of trust. Some extracts I did indeed give from them in a book which I published in 1882, and even now I content myself with indicating the drift of those long conversations by post which were the consequence of the two hundred miles which divided me from my friend.

If, as I have not hesitated to show in an earlier chapter, Rossetti gave me on occasion the encouragement of his warmest praise, he did not shrink from playing the part of mentor also, censuring, particularly, a tendency to involution in style, the abnormal search after "phrase" and the "outstanding word," which, strange as I find it to remember, was at that time a disfiguring characteristic of my writing. Prose, he would say, might be fervid and vivid, but it ought to be simple and direct, rarely calling attention to itself, never breaking the rhythmic flow by forced or foreign expression or yet carrying it on for the mere sake of effect.

"Surely," he said, "you are strong enough to be English pure and simple. I am sure I could write a hundred essays on all possible subjects (I once did project a series under the title 'Essays written in the intervals of Elephantiasis, Hydrophobia, and Penal Servitude'), without once experiencing the 'aching void,' which is filled by such words as 'mythopoeic,' and 'anthropomorphism.' I do not find life long enough to know in the least what they mean. They are both very long and very ugly indeed – the latter only suggesting to me a vampire or a somnambulant cannibal."

He was equally severe on my tendency to quote the opinions of certain journals that had spoken well of me. The criticism of good critics might be good, and therefore good to quote, but much criticism was bad, and therefore it was bad to mention it.

"Really, I cannot but say," he said, "that the last page of your new pamphlet is sadly disfigured by the names of London prints which are conducted by the lowest gangs – at least, I will answer for *one* being so. You have begun, as you tell me, and as I somewhat divine, in a scrambling literary way, and the sooner you shake off all such connections the nearer you will be to your goal. No need to take any notice of this, in any way. It is a finger-post which only asks to be followed in silence. Indeed I will *ask* you not to answer."

Having to some extent cast in his lot with me, he was irritated by any loss of what he thought becoming dignity on my part, and not only remonstrated against my publishing articles in magazines which he called "farragoes of absolute garbage," but was even reluctant to allow me, when I was about to edit an anthology of sonnets, to write to the poets who were to be asked to contribute.

"I must say I rather doubt the wisdom of writing

without introduction to such men as you mention. A superior man runs the risk, by doing so, of being confounded with those who are perpetually directing correspondence to anyone whose name they have heard – and the bibliographic and autograph-hunting tribe whose name is legion. I do not mean that such an application as yours could *rightly* be classed with these, but I know the sort of exclamation that rises to the lips of a man as much beset by strangers as (say) Swinburne, when he opens a letter and sees a new name at the end of it."

He was hardly less irritated by a tendency of mine to set the manner of a work higher than its substance, to glorify style as if it were a thing apart from subject.

"You have too great a habit of speaking of a special octave, sestette, or line. Conception, my boy, FUNDAMENTAL BRAINWORK, that is what makes the difference in all art. Work your metal as much as you like, but first take care that it is gold and worth working. A Shakespearean sonnet is better than the most perfect in form because Shakespeare wrote it."

"But, I hope you won't think that I am everlastingly playing mentor," he said, and to lift up my heart after so many packs of the wet blanket, he wrote, about a new lecture on the scarcely confluent elements of "Politics and Art": "It is abundantly rich in spirit and animated truth, and in powerful language, too, when required. It must do you high credit wherever seen, and when you are able to enlarge your sphere, I look to you as destined to rank among the coming teachers of men."

All the same he was too discreet to accept the dedication of this same lecture, when I came to print it, though the letter in which he declined was touching, and, I think, sincere:

"I must admit at all hazards that my friends consider me exceptionally averse to politics; and I suppose I must be, for I have never read a Parliamentary debate in my life! At the same time, I must add that, among those whose opinions I most value, some think me not altogether wrong when I venture to speak of the momentary momentousness and eternal futility of many noisiest questions. However, you must simply view me as a nonentity in any practical relation to such matters. You have spoken but too generously of a sonnet of mine in the lecture just received. I have written a few others of the sort (which, by-the-bye, would not prove me a Tory), but felt no vocation – perhaps no right – to print them. I have always reproached myself as sorely amenable to the condemnation of a very fine poem by Barberino on 'Sloth against Sin', which I translated in the Dante volume. Sloth, alas, has but too much to answer for with me; and is one of the reasons (though I will not say the only one) why I have always fallen back on quality instead of quantity in the little I have ever done. I think often with Coleridge:

> Sloth jaundiced all: and from my graspless hand
> Drop friendship's precious pearls like hour-glass sand.
> I weep, yet stoop not: the faint anguish flows,
> A dreamy pang in morning's feverish doze."

Though my beginnings had been scrambling ones, it was my own fault now if my literary education was not more thorough and even more systematic than any school or university could have given me. Notwithstanding the calls of my ordinary occupation, I was reading as much as six, eight, and even ten hours a day, and corresponding constantly on the subject of my reading with a man of genius whose knowledge of literature was very wide, and whose instinct for excellence was very sure. Our studies were, of course, mainly English, but I think they covered the whole range of what was best, from Shakespeare and even the less-known Elizabethan poets, through Steel, Savage, Goldsmith, Johnson, Cowper, Fielding, and Richardson, to the writers of the "Lake," "Cockney," and "Satanic" schools, coming down to our own day with Tennyson andBrowning, and covering some of the forgotten geniuses of yesterday, such as Smart and Wells.

Rossetti's letters to me, which are equal in quantity to the contents of a very large volume, are studded with names familiar and unfamiliar, which show how vigorously, throughout the years in which he had been occupied chiefly with painting, he must have burrowed in the bypaths as well as laboured in the highways of literature; and when I remember the disadvantages of my own beginning I must not forget that for two and a half years I had the daily coaching of Rossetti's forty years of reading and the constant guidance of his fine selective instinct. That of itself ought to have been a literary education of the highest kind, though it was not then that I so regarded it, nor do I suppose for a moment that Rossetti himself looked at it in any such light. I see, with some amusement, that in the course of our correspondence I sometimes withstood his judgments and occasionally remonstrated against his "prejudices."

Thus I protested that he was radically unjust to

Wordsworth, whom he had not the patience to read except in fugitive passages taken at random, and he answered:

"I grudge Wordsworth every vote he gets. . . . No one regards the great Ode with more special and unique homage than I do, as a thing absolutely alone of its kind among all greatest things. I cannot say that anything else of his with which I have ever been familiar (and I suffer from long disuse of all familiarity with him), seems to me at all on a level with this."

We were on common ground, however, in the worship of Coleridge. "The three greatest English imaginations," he said, "are Shakespeare, Coleridge, and Shelley," and he never tired of extolling the beauties of "Christabel".

"Of course the first part is so immeasurably beyond the second that one feels Charles Lamb's view was right, and the poem should have been abandoned at that point. The passage on Sundered Friendship is one of the masterpieces of the language, but no doubt was written quite separately and then fitted into 'Christabel' – the two lines about 'Roland and Sir Leoline' are simply an intrusion and an outrage."

Another of Rossetti's references to "Christabel" is interesting for the peep it affords into the home of his boyhood, where English books, it seems, were few.

"There are, I believe, many continuations of 'Christabel.' Tupper did one! I myself saw a continuation in childhood, long before I saw the original, and was all agog to see it for years. Our household was all of Italian, not English environment, however, and it was only when I went to school later that I began to ransack bookstalls."

With sufficient audacity, I came into collision with Rossetti again over Chatterton, whom I was not at first prepared to regard with special reverence, apart from the fact that against tremendous odds and at seventeen years of age he had written anything that deserved to be remembered at all; but nothing would suffice for Rossetti but that I should go down on my knees and worship the author of the African Eclogues.

"I assure you," he said, "Chatterton was as great as any English poet whatever, and might absolutely, had he lived, have proved the only man in England's theatre of imagination who could have bandied parts with Shakespeare."

At my insinuation that perhaps part of one's interest in Chatterton had its origin in the fact that he was a bit of a blackguard, and not so much in admiration of his poems as in surprise that a boy of sixteen should have written them, Rossetti, as was most natural, fired up warmly:

"I must protest finally that the man who says that cannot know what criticism means. Chatterton was an absolute and untarnished hero. . . . Surely a boy up to eighteen may be pardoned for exercising his faculty if he happens to be one among millions who can use grown men as his toys. Certainly that most vigorous passage commencing:

'Interest, thou universal God of men,'

reads startlingly, and comes in a questionable shape. What is the answer to its enigmatical aspect? Why, that he *meant* it, and that all would mean it as his age, who had his power, his daring, and his hunger."

I was on safer ground with Rossetti when we began

to write about Keats, "the lovely and beloved Keats."

"You say an excellent thing," he said, "when you ask, 'Where can we look for more poetry per page than Keats gives us?' I shall look forward with very great interest to your essay on Keats."

And when the Keats paper was sent to him he made up for many critical denunciations by the warmest sympathy.

"I have this minute at last read the Keats paper, and return it. It is excellent throughout, and the closing passage is very finely worded. . . . You quote some of Keats's sayings. One of the most characteristic, I think, is in a letter to Haydon: 'I value more the privilege of seeing great things in loneliness than the fame of a prophet.' . . . Keats wrote to Shelley: 'You, I am sure, will forgive me for sincerely remarking that you might curb your magnanimity, and be more of an artist, and load every rift of your subject with ore.' Cheeky! But not so much amiss. Poetry and no prophecy, however, must have come of that mood; and no pulpit would have held Keats's wings."

In this way the Rossetti correspondence had, with great profit to me, been going on for a considerable time, when my personal affairs reached an acute but not altogether unexpected crisis. My long-standing grievance against my everyday occupation as a builder's draughtsman was, in spite of the never-failing indulgence of my employer, brought to a head by another attack of illness. The symptoms were sufficiently alarming this time; but although satisfied that I had received my death-warrant, I said nothing to anybody except the doctor and Rossetti, to whom, by this time, I was in the habit of telling everything. Rossetti replied with his usual solicitude, coupled with his customary remonstrance.

Grave as the issue certainly was, it is almost amusing to me to remember that, being convinced that my failure of health was mainly due to the zeal with which for several years I had been burning the candle at both ends, it did not occur to me for a moment to put it out at the end that was apparently least necessary to my material welfare. My easy work in the building yard made me my living, while my hard work with my books made me nothing at all; but I take it to be an evidence of how the itch for writing will conquer all practical considerations, and perhaps evidence, also, of a certain natural vocation, that when I came to choose between those two, it was the living that had to go.

It is also amusing to me to remember that when I announced to Rossetti that the time had come for me to cut away from business, and to sink or swim in an effort to live by my pen, having no literary connections at that time that were safe for sixpence, it was he – he who had predicted such certain success for me – who was thrown into a state of the greatest alarm. But even Rossetti's alarm did not alarm me, and, spurred perhaps by secret and increasing fear of a disease from which more than one member of my family had died, I left my architectural employment rather abruptly, as I now see, notwithstanding various kind overtures from James Bromley, the archaeologist, my employer and my friend.

On seeing that I was fully resolved to burn my boats, Rossetti proposed that I should pitch my tent with him in London.

"I feel greatly interested," he said, "in your prospects and intentions, and at this writing I can see no likelihood of my not remaining in the mind that, in case of your coming to London, your quarters should be taken up here. The house is big enough for two, even if they meant to be strangers to each other. You would have your own rooms, and we should meet just when we pleased. You have got a sufficient inkling of my exceptional habits not to be scared by them. It is true, at times my health and spirits are variable; but I am sure we should not be squabbling."

I hesitated to take advantage of such a one-sided arrangement as Rossetti proposed, and in order to overcome my reluctance, he began to protest that he, too, was far from well, and that my presence in his house might be helpful in various ways.

"You must not be anxious on my account," he said. "But any cause whatever which should bring you (but not to your own injury) to my door, would be welcome in result."

CHAPTER IX

WE SELL "DANTE'S DREAM"

In writing this book it is equally outside my purpose and beyond my power to deal with Rossetti's activities as a painter. But as I was possibly the first instrument in making his greatest picture known to the world, it may not be improper that I should tell the somewhat amusing story of the struggle we had to get it out of the artist's studio.

In an earlier chapter I have said that I saw "Dante's Dream" first on my second visit to Rossetti's studio, when I was still living in Liverpool. On my way home I conceived the idea that a fitting place for it would be the municipal gallery in Liverpool, and in due course I mentioned the matter to the Chairman of the Liverpool Council. He was deeply interested and raised the question at a meeting of his Committee; whereupon a sub-committee of three was appointed to go up to Rossetti's house and negotiate the purchase.

But, by the unluckiest of unlucky misadventures, one of the three appointed was the very man who had presided over my lecture, when he had said that Rossetti (who painted women chiefly) was "the greatest *animal* painter in England." On hearing of his appointment Rossetti flatly refused to receive him, and wrote to me in great indignation: "What do you mean by shunting my enemies into my house?" Upon this I prevailed on the Chairman to go up alone and try to make peace with Rossetti. The good man did so, and succeeded. Rossetti wrote me an amusing account of his surrender:

"S–, said R–, although eccentric and irresponsible, was really a good fellow at bottom. I was quite tractable. I did not mention that if — came here he had better take care that the place at which he was a good fellow did not get kicked."

A little later the Committee arrived in London, the terms of the purchase were concluded, and everything went well until the moment came to arrange for the placing of the picture in the Municipal Art Gallery. Then it was suddenly discovered that, by the standing orders of the Liverpool Corporation, no picture could be purchased for the city except out of the annual autumn exhibition. Rossetti objected again. For countless years he had never exhibited a picture, and whatever the consequences he would not exhibit one now. Liverpool must buy the picture before they exhibited it, or they should not buy it at all.

The Committee called in my assistance. I was to go up to Rossetti and explain that the standing order was no more than a matter of form. I went up, and nearly all Rossetti's friends, his brother, Watts, Shields, and, I think, Ford Madox Brown, joined me with Rossetti in his studio. We found Rossetti utterly unyielding. The position was both ludicrous and serious. Liverpool (as I knew) wanted the picture very earnestly, while Rossetti (as we all knew) wanted the money; but neither could nor would budge an inch. All of us in turn tried our powers of persuasion on Rossetti in vain. I remember that I said that my friend the Chairman had promised me that he would "star" the picture as purchased the moment the first member of the public had passed the turnstile, and that I would return to see that he kept his promise. Rossetti would not listen to any of us. For reasons which he thought good and sufficient he had not exhibited a picture since he was a very young man, and he would not break the rule of his life now, even if the picture were never sold at all and he had to starve as the consequence.

We were in a quandary. At length there was silence. I went out of the room. Suddenly a simple idea occurred to me, and coming back, I cried: "Rossetti, give the picture to *me* and *I* will exhibit it and sell it to Liverpool." The friends shouted as one man: "The very thing! Splendid! An inspiration! Caine's got it!"

Rossetti agreed; the great picture became technically mine; I sent it to Liverpool; it was exhibited; Liverpool sent me a cheque for the purchase-price (£1,550) and I took it up to Rossetti, who was in bed, and flung it down on his counterpane, saying: "There you are, Gabriel! We've done the trick, you see!" Rossetti laughed. I think he was both amused and grateful.

But difficulties of other sorts came to Rossetti on the head of this, and one of the most serious of them concerned the tenancy of his house, the landlords demanding the right to take away his large garden, almost the only refuge he had had for fresh air and exercise during the long years in which he had lived the life of a hermit. From this further embarrassment he was rescued by Watts, who was a solicitor as well as a man of letters, and was as ready as any of us to sacrifice every ounce of his energy and great tact to his friend.

During the first half of 1881, in the midst of these "bedevilments," Rossetti had been collecting, revising, and finally printing and correcting the proofs of his second volume of poems, and partly as a consequence of his increasing anxieties he was now, unknown to his friends, exceeding terribly in the use of the insidious drug which had long been undermining his health. So it came about that when, in the early summer, under the mistaken idea that my own health was seriously undermined, I left Liverpool for good and went up to the Vale of St. John in Cumberland, resolved, if I shook off my trouble, to toil early and late, and live in a cottage on oatmeal porridge and barley bread, rather than give up my intention of becoming a man of letters, Rossetti, also influenced by considerations of health, came to the conclusion that if I would not come to him, he would go to me. Scarcely had I settled in my remote quarters, when he wrote that he must soon leave London; that he was wearied out and unable to sleep; that if he could only reach my secluded vale he would breathe a purer air, mentally as well as physically.

"They are now really setting about the building at the back here. I do not know what my plans may be. Suppose I were to ask you to come to town in a fortnight from now, and perhaps I returning with you for a while into the country, would that be feasible to you?"

The idea of my going up to London and bringing Rossetti back with me to Cumberland became a settled scheme, and towards the beginning of August he wrote:

"I will hope to see you in town on Saturday next, unless an earlier day suits decidedly better. We will then set sail in one boat. I am rather anxious as to having become perfectly deaf on the right side of my head. Partial approaches to this have sometimes occurred to me and passed away, so I will not be too much troubled. . . . I am getting the rooms cleared out for your reception."

In due course I arrived in London, and was received with the utmost warmth. The cheery "Hulloa" greeted me again as I entered the studio, and then Rossetti, feebler of step, I thought, than before, led the way to the apartments he had prepared for me.

My sitting-room was the room to the left of the hall, facing the green dining-room, with a huge sofa and two huge chairs in an apple-blossom chintz, a table, a black oak cabinet and a number of small photographs of Rossetti's designs for pictures in plain oak frames, all now at my home in the Isle of Man. It had been occupied in turn by Meredith and by Swinburne in the days when they had lived under the same roof with Rossetti, and henceforward it was to be mine for my permanent home in London. In this way I drifted into my place as Rossetti's housemate, and very soon I realized what the position involved.

CHAPTER X

ROSSETTI AND HIS FRIENDS

Rossetti was now a changed man. He was distinctly less inclined to corpulence, his eyes were less bright, and when he walked to and fro in the studio, as it was his habit to do at intervals of about an hour, it was with a laboured, side-long motion that I had not previously observed. Half sensible of an anxiety which I found it difficult to conceal, he paused for an instant in the midst of these melancholy perambulations, and asked how he struck me as to health. More frankly than wisely I answered: "Less well than formerly." It was an unlucky remark, for Rossetti's secret desire at that moment was to conceal his lowering state even from himself.

He had written his "King's Tragedy" since I had stayed with him before, and I think he wished me to believe that the emotional strain involved in the production of the poem had been chiefly to blame for his reduced condition. Casting himself on the couch with a look of exhaustion, he told me that the ballad had taken a great deal out of him. "It was as though my life ebbed out with it," he said. Undoubtedly the weight of his work was still upon him. Even his voice seemed to have lost something in quality, and to have diminished in compass also, for when he spoke he conveyed the idea of speaking as much to himself as to me.

In actual fact, however, making allowances for the strain of work as well as the worry of domestic disturbances, his physical retrogression was undoubtedly due in great part to recent excess in the use of the pernicious drug. With that excess had come a certain moral as well as bodily decline. I thought I perceived that he was more than ever enslaved by the painful delusion that there was a conspiracy against him; more than ever under the influence of intermittent waves of morbid suspicion of nearly everybody with whom he came in contact.

Right or wrong, this diagnosis of Rossetti's case was perhaps the one thing that enabled me, as a young fellow out of the fresh air of the commonplace world, to do the poet some good - to cheer and strengthen him, and to bring for a time a little happiness into his life. Down to the moment of my coming he had for years rarely been outside the doors of his great, gloomy house – certainly never afoot, and only in closed carriages with his friends; but on the second night of my stay I marched boldly into the studio, announced my intention of taking a walk on the Chelsea Embankment, and, without a qualm, asked Rossetti to accompany me. To my amazement he consented, saying: "Well, upon my word, really I think I will." Every night for a week afterwards I induced him to repeat the unfamiliar experiment.

But now I recall with emotion and some remorse the scene and circumstance of those nightly walks; the Embankment almost dark, with its gas-lamps far apart, and generally silent at our late hour, except for an occasional footfall on the pavement under the tall houses opposite; the black river flowing noiselessly behind the low wall and gurgling under the bridge; and then Rossetti in his slouch hat, with its broad brim pulled down low on his forehead as if to conceal his face, lurching along with a heavy, uncertain step, breathing audibly, looking at nothing, and hardly speaking at all. From these nightly perambulations he would return home utterly exhausted, and throwing himself on the couch, remain prostrate for nearly an hour.

I seem to remember that on one of our walks along the Embankment late at night we passed in the half-darkness two figures which bore a certain resemblance to our own – an old man in a Scotch plaid, accompanied by a slight young woman in a sort of dolman. The old man was forging along sturdily with the help of a stick, and the young woman appeared to be making some effort to keep pace with him. It was Carlyle with his niece, and I caught but one glimpse of them as, out on the same errand as ourselves, they went off in the other direction.[1]

Although it was understood between us that I had come up to London with the express purpose of taking Rossetti back with me to Cumberland, he seemed to be in no hurry for our departure. Day by day, and week by week, with all the ingenuity of his native irresolution, he devised reasons for delay; and thus a month passed before we began to make a move.

---

1 On second thoughts I conclude that this must have been in 1880, but I am not altogether sure.

Meantime we commenced our career together under the same roof, and to me it was both interesting and helpful. Rossetti's habits of life were indeed, as he said, exceptional, and in some respects they seemed to turn the world topsy-turvy. I am convinced that at this time only the necessity of securing a certain short interval of daylight by which it was possible to paint, prevailed with him to get up before the middle of the afternoon. Rising about noon, and breakfasting in his little ante-room (an enormous breakfast of six eggs or half-a-dozen kidneys), he would come down to the studio and sit steadily at his easel for three or four hours, with two or three intervals of perhaps a quarter of an hour each for walking to and fro.

"I believe in doing a little work every day, and doing it as well as I can," he would say.

When the light began to fail he would come to my sitting-room to see how I was "getting along", an errand which invariably resulted in our going back together to the studio and talking until dinner-time.

His talk at this period was hardly ever personal. I was now, by the invitation of the Chairman of the Library Committee, preparing a course of lectures to be delivered in Liverpool during the autumn, and our conversation was nearly always on the subject of my studies. This was the prose literature of the latter half of the eighteenth century in England (chiefly Fielding, Richardson, Smollett, and Defoe), and Rossetti threw himself into my work with as much ardour as if it had been his own. I remember that he did not strike me as particularly well read in fiction, but he had a faculty I had never seen in anybody else – that of knowing things without taking the trouble to learn them, of seeing things without looking at them, of understanding things without thinking of them – a faculty beyond and apart from talent, and having little or nothing to do with industry. Remembering the bright light of Rossetti's intellect, I am by no means sure that of all the men of genius I have ever known he did not stand alone.

We dined about half-past eight, generally in the studio and often without company, sat up till two or three, and then went to bed, with our candles in our hands and volumes of "Clarissa" or "Tom Jones" under our arms.

Nights of such loneliness were frequently broken, however, by the society of Rossetti's friends, and during the weeks of our waiting I came to know one by one the few men and women who remained of the poet's intimate circle. There was his brother William, a staid and rather silent man, at that time in the Civil Service, growing elderly and apparently encompassed by family cares, but coming to Cheyne Walk every Monday night with unfailing regularity and a brotherly loyalty that never flagged. There was Theodore Watts (afterwards Watts-Dunton), most intimate of Rossetti's friends, a short man, then in the prime of life, with a great head and brilliant eyes. There was Frederic Shields, the painter, on the sunny side of middle age, enthusiastic, spontaneous, almost spasmodic. There was (about once a week) William Bell Scott, poet and painter, very emotional, very sensitive, a little embittered, a tall old man who had lost his hair and wore a wig which somewhat belied his face. There was Ford Madox Brown, a handsome elderly man with a long whitening beard, a solid figure with a firm step, a dignified manner, and a sententious style of speech. Then there was William Sharp (now known as Fiona Macleod), a young fellow in his early twenties, very bright, very winsome, very lively, very lovable, very Scotch, always telling, in what Rossetti called "the unknown tongue," exaggerated and incredible stories which made him laugh uproariously, but were never intended to be believed. And then (less frequently) there was the blind poet, Philip Bourke Marston, a pathetic figure, slack and untidy, with large lips and pale cheeks, silent, gloomy, and perhaps morbid.

These constituted the inner circle of Rossetti's friends. Outside this inner circle there were various writers and painters who would have joined us, if they had been *as welcome as willing*. Rossetti's closer friends came at varying intervals: Watts twice or thrice a week, Shields more rarely, Brown on the occasions of his holidays in London from his work on the frescoes in the Town Hall at Manchester: Sharp and Marston now and then. Once or twice during the weeks of our waiting there were visits from the ladies of Rossetti's family, his mother, a gentle, sweet-faced old lady, in a long sealskin coat (the treasured gift of the poet), and his sister Christina, a woman in middle life, with a fine, intellectual face, noticeably large and somewhat protrusive eyes, a pleasant smile and a quiet manner, but a power of clear-cut incisive speech which gave an astonishing effect of mental strength. Finally, there were rare and valued visits from Mrs. William Morris, the subject of many of Rossetti's pictures, no longer young but still wondrously beautiful, with the grand, sad face which the painter has made immortal in those three-quarter-length pictures which, for wealth of sublime and mysterious suggestion, unaided by dramatic design, are probably unique in the art of the world.

I never met her. She was the only intimate friend of Rossetti whom I did not meet. As often as she came he would write a little note and send it out to me, saying: "The lady I spoke about has arrived and will stay with me to dinner. In these circumstances I will ask you to be good enough to dine in your own room to-night." Naturally, I respected to the end the sincerity of what I then believed, and still believe, to have been from first to last the most beautiful of friendships, although it deprived me of the acquaintance of the one member of his circle whom, most of all, and for more reasons than I can give, I desired to meet.

Naturally, it could not be altogether a desolate house in which such men and women gathered at intervals around one of the most extraordinary personalities of the age, and notwithstanding the graudal lowering of Rossetti's health, we had our cheerful hours together. I recall the dinners in the studio in the midst of the easels, four or five of us at most; the big pipes of macaroni (brought from Soho and larger than any I have ever since seen in Italy) with which we always began; the Chianti and water with which we washed them down; the game of Limericks we played about the table, everybody taking his turn, for it was trick easily learned (the unhappy subject being usually the friend who had not turned up), and the peals of laughter that rang through the room as Rossetti's rhyme, aflame with satire that was not always without the power to sting, fell on us like a thunderbolt. Rabelaisian? No, and never for one moment irreverent to the dead. Not Keats himself ever felt more humble in the memory of great men. To have done anything supremely well, in any form of human activity, but especially with the pen or the brush, was to command the solemnity of his respect. We all took our tone from him – I, being the youngest, especially. Nearly half a century has passed since those great nights in the studio at Cheyne Walk, yet they are with me still.

But I should do poor service to the truth if I made it appear that even after my long correspondence with him my life under his roof was one of perpetual blue skies and unbroken sunshine. There were clouds that were dark and, to me, rather heavy. They were almost entirely from outside our own united and devoted circle. One of them came with a remarkable man, whom I will not further identify than to say that he was from Liverpool, where I had heard of him frequently and not always to his advantage. There could have been little in common between this man and Rossetti, except that he brought an atmosphere of great adventures in a big world of which the poet and painter, in his long seclusion from life, knew little or nothing. And then, being rich, he was a frequent buyer of Rossetti's pictures and, therefore, a person to be encouraged, not to say cultivated.

I saw him first when he dined with us soon after my arrival at Rossetti's house, and, having regard to his humble origin, I found him an unaccountable dandy of the type of the earliest days of Disraeli – wearing, with his morning clothes, a frilled shirt and bows on his patent-leather shoes. After dinner he talked vivaciously and, by evil chance, chiefly of his career in Liverpool. I cannot charge my memory with everything he said, but the substance of it was a somewhat flamboyant account of how he had begun his business life by entering his office as office-boy and ended it by turning his master out of doors.

It pained me to see that Rossetti found a certain delight in the heartless narrative as a record of relentless power. Before it was finished I rose and left the studio. I did not return to it until the visitor had gone, and then Rossetti took me sternly to task.

"Why did you leave the studio while So-and-So was talking?" he asked, and I answered, perhaps with unnecessary vehemence:

"Because I could not listen any longer to his infamous story."

"But why not? . . ." he cried.

"Do you ask me that, Rossetti? Besides, you cannot but remember that I, too, come from Liverpool."

I have spoken of the writers outside our circle who would have been eager to enter it if they had been as welcome as willing, and now, not long after my arrival, it came to my knowledge that Rossetti was hearing what they were saying of the young fellow from the country who had superseded them without having asked. Once, at least, Rossetti gave me some account of what they were saying. They knew nothing whatever about me, therefore I feel no shame in repeating their charges – that I was a mediocre parasite, ignorant, illiterate and entirely destitute of knowledge of literature, his secretary, his personal attendant, his – God knows what! Why Rossetti told me this I cannot remember. I did not defend myself. But, with a beating heart, I made it clear to him that I was in his house because of the affection I felt for him and the affection

I believed he felt for me, but that if at any time I became conscious of any failure of this on either side it would not take me an hour to go, even if it had to be to the humblest back room in the meanest back street.

What Rossetti said in reply I cannot permit my pen to write; but as for the serpentine outsiders who tried to belittle me in his eyes when I was young, unknown and poor, I hear no call of modesty which forbids me to say that within five years I had wiped every man of them off the map.

"Gabriel knew what he was doing."

Apart from incidents like these, not many echoes of the outer world came to us in that closed circle of Rossetti's house, for there was a kind of silent acquiescence in the idea that the affairs of everyday life were proscribed. I cannot remember that we talked politics at all, or that a daily newspaper ever entered our doors. A criminal trial, with a mystery attached to it, would awaken Rossetti's keenest interest and set his amazing powers of deduction to work; but social movements had small value in his eyes, and even religious agitations rarely moved him. I remember that a little of my native Puritanism took me one Sunday morning to hear Spurgeon, the Nonconformist preacher, at the moment when he was in the fires of what was called his "down-grade" crusade, but I tried in vain to interest Rossetti in the burning propaganda.

Literary doings, and in a less degree artistic ones also, commanded Rossetti's attention always, for his house was a hotbed of intellectual activity, and I recall, in particular, his anxiety to know what was being published and discussed. A young poet, who was just then attracting attention by certain peculiarities of personal behaviour and a series of cartoons in which he was caricatured by Du Maurier in *Punch*, sent Rossetti his first book of poems, a volume bound in parchment and inscribed, I think, in gold. This was Oscar Wilde, and I remember Rossetti's quick recognition of the gifts that underlay a good deal of amusing affectation.

The air was at that time full of stories of Whistler's pecuniary distresses, and I remember, too, a string of ridiculous anecdotes which Rossetti used to tell of "Jimmy's" eccentricities. Then there was Swinburne, a figure that seemed to be always hovering about Rossetti's house (though during my time his body was never present there), so constantly was he discussed either by Watts, by Rossetti, or by myself. But of other and still more intimate friends of earlier life – Ruskin, Morris, Holman Hunt, and Burne-Jones – nothing was seen and hardly anything was said; and of this fact I can offer no explanation here – none, at least, except by side-light derived from Rossetti's great love and frequent repetition of Coleridge's "Work without Hope".

Rossetti's second volume of poems, "Ballads and Sonnets" was published during our weeks of waiting. The book had a great reception. If, once again, there was at first a measure of adverse criticism, Rossetti, in his failing health, was allowed to know nothing about that either. All he saw in the name of criticism was a noble and brilliant appreciation by Watts-Dunton (*Athenaeum*), which, as I remember, brought the tears to his eyes when he read it, a fine analysis by Professor Dowden (*Academy*), and an article, all adoration, by me. Beyond this, and the general impression we all conveyed to him that his book was being magnificently received, Rossetti had no other knowledge of the fate of his new book than came to him in the substantial form of his publishers' cheques, which seemed to me, at that time, very large.

Rossetti might have been expected to find joy in the fact that in one month, by the simultaneous production of two masterpieces, he had again become illustrious in two arts, but it would wrong the truth to say that he gave any particular sign of satisfaction. I cannot recall that he showed a real interest in the reception of his picture, or that the fate of his new book gave him a moment's apparent uneasiness.

If I had not heard of the feverish watchfulness with which he had followed the fortunes of his earlier volume, I should have concluded that the absence of anxiety about his second book was due to a calm reliance on its strength. But the intensity of Rossetti's sensitiveness to any breath of criticism was as great as ever, and it is more than probable that the same shrinking from public observation which had made him a hermit made him shut out of his consciousness any influence that might possibly bring him pain.

I remember that one morning, not long after the publication of the book, coming unexpectedly into my sitting-room and seeing on the table a copy of a well-known weekly journal lying open at a page in which some purblind person, reviewing the "Ballads," began, "It is difficult to determine exactly what position the author of these poems fills in the category of secondary poets". Rossetti fired up at me again for "shunting his enemies into his house", and then went off to his studio in a towering rage. The unlucky article was no doubt foolish enough as criticism in a leading place of a book which gave proof of one of the great poets of the century, but I thought it was necessary to look elsewhere than to the natural irritability of the poetic nature for the reason of Rossetti's want of manliness in meeting with one more evidence of the perpetual presence of the egregious ass.

Unfortunately, it was not necessary to look far. Day by day, or night by night, prompted, perhaps, by the desire to suppress the nervousness created by his domestic worries, the sale of his pictures and the publication of his book, Rossetti was giving way more and more to indulgence in the accursed drug; and not all our efforts to keep painful facts from his knowledge, nor yet our innocent scheming to fill his gloomy house with sunshine, availed to bring any real happiness into his life.

I remember that one day his brother William's wife (a daughter of Madox Brown) sent her children to Cheyne Walk on a visit to their uncle, thinking, no doubt, to brighten him up by their cheerful presence. But beyond a momentary welcome from the poet as he sat in the studio, and a constrained greeting from the little ones, nothing came of the innocent artifice, and Rossetti heard no more of them than their happy laughter as they romped upstairs and downstairs through the rest of the house.

August had slid into September while we waited in London without obvious purpose, and it was now plainly apparent to all Rossetti's friends that, out of regard both to the condition of his health and the time of the year, he must go back to Cumberland with me immediately, if he was to go at all. Once out of this atmosphere of gloom, of anxiety and of irritation, we thought his spirits would revive and his physical weakness disappear.

Infinite were the efforts that had to be made, and countless the precautions that had to be taken (including the commission to my care only of a boxful of bottles of chloral) before Rossetti could be induced to set out; but at length, after a farewell visit to Torrington Square to say good-bye to his mother and sister, we found ourselves, we two and the nurse (an old friend, of whom I may say something later), one evening in September, at Euston Station, sitting behind the drawn blinds of a special saloon carriage that was labelled for Keswick, and packed with as many baskets and bags, as many books and artist's trappings, as would have lasted for an absence of a year.

CHAPTER XI

FIRST WEEKS IN THE VALE

To paint a portrait of Rossetti as he was when I lived with him in the last year of his life is to present a very complex personality, having many conflicting impulses, many contradictory manifestations; and if by any revelation of truth, I can account for the want of harmony in the poet's character, and in the impression it made upon observers, I shall perhaps do something to recover the real Rossetti from the misrepresentations of detractors who hated him, and of the admirers who did not understand him.

I have not concealed my conviction that the less noble side of Rossetti came of prolonged indulgence in a pernicious drug, and once again I cannot, and will not, attempt to omit an illustration of the corrupting influence of his unfortunate habit. Our journey to Cumberland was a long and tiresome one. The man who could not sleep in a muffled bedroom fronting an open garden was hardly likely to sleep in a rumbling and jolting railway train, but towards midnight I gave Rossetti his usual dose, and went to sleep.

I awoke when the train stopped at Penrith, and the dawn was breaking, but Rossetti was still lying where I had left him. Something suggested that I should look in my handbag, and to my distress I discovered that one of two bottles of chloral I had left in it had gone.

It was six o'clock when we reached the little way-side station (Threlkeld) that was the end of our journey, and there we got into a carriage which was to drive us through the Vale of St. John to the Legberth-waite end of it. The morning was calm; the mountains looked grand and noble with the mists floating over their crowns; nothing could be heard but the call of awakening cattle, the rumble of the cataracts that were far away, and the surge of the rivers that were near. Rossetti was all but indifferent to our surroundings, or displayed only such fitful interest in them as must have been affected out of a kindly desire to please me. He said the chloral I had given him on the journey was in his eyes so that he could not rightly see, and as soon as we reached the house that was to be our home, he declared his intention of going to bed.

I saw him to his room and then left him im-mediately, perceiving he was anxious to dismiss me, but returning a moment afterwards with some urgent message, I opened his door without knocking, and came suddenly upon him in the act of drinking the contents of the bottle of chloral I had missed from the bag.

It would be impossible for me, even now at this dis-tance of time, to convey any sense of the crushing humiliation of this incident, of the abject degradation which the habit of chloral had brought about in an in-genuous, frank, and noble nature. It was not then, however, that Rossetti himself had any consciousness of this. Indeed, I thought there was even something almost cruel in the laugh with which he received my nervous protest. But afterwards – when the effects of the drug were gone and he realized the pain he had caused, the fear he had created, the hours I had walked on tiptoe in the corridor outside his door listening for the sound of his breathing, in terror lest it should stop – the true man showed himself, the real Rossetti, and he said, as he did again and again on other occasions:

"I wish you were really my son, for though I should have no right to treat you so, I should at least have some reason to expect your forgiveness."

At such moments of more than needful solicitude for one's acutest sensibilities, Rossetti was absolutely irresistible.

Although he had consumed, since we left London, a quantity of chloral that would have been sufficient to destroy, perhaps, all the other members of our little household put together, Rossetti awoke fresh and in good spirits towards the middle of the afternoon, breakfasted heartily, and then took a turn about the house which was intended to be our home for at least a couple of months to come. It was a modest place named Fisher Ghyll, having a guest-house in front consisting of three sitting-rooms and as many bed-rooms, and a group of farm buildings at the back. Standing in what may be called the estuary of the valley, where the Vale of St. John empties into the dale of Thirlmere, it had the purple heights of Blencathra to the north, the scraggy rocks of the Dunmail Raise to the south, the Styx Pass and the brant sides of Helvellyn behind it, and before it the wooded slopes of Golden Howe, the climbing road to Keswick and the pathway of the setting sun. Not a sound about the house except the occasional voice of a child or bark of a dog, the splash of falling water, the bleating of sheep, the echo of the axe of the woodman who was thinning the neighbouring plantation, and the horn of the mail-coach that passed morning and evening from the little market-town five miles away.

Rossetti was delighted. Here, at least, he might bury the memory of a hundred "bogies" that had vexed him; here, in this exhilarating air, he might recover the health he had lost in the close atmosphere of his studio in London; and here, too, amidst the vivid scenery, so wonderfully awakening to the imagination, so full of poetic appeal and ghostly legend, he might turn again to the romantic ballad which he had expected to write among such surroundings.

Next day he was exceptionally well, and astounded me by the proposal that we should ascend Golden Howe together – the little mountain, of perhaps a thousand feet, that stands at the head of Thirlmere. With never a hope, on my part, of reaching the top, we set out for that purpose; but, weak as he had been a few days before, Rossetti actually accomplished the task he proposed for himself, going up slowly, little by little, through the ferns and the fir trees, with their rabbits and red-tailed squirrels, and then sitting for a long hour on the summit. It was a marvellous picture that lay about us, with the lake below and the un-dulating mountain tops above. Rossetti was much im-pressed.

"I'm not one of those who care about scenery, but this is marvellous, and the colour is wonderful," he said.

His spirits were high, and when, on beginning our descent, he lost his footing and slithered some distance through the bracken before I could stop him, he only laughed and said:

"Don't be afraid, I always go up on my feet and come down on a broader basis."

He painted a little during those first quiet days in Cumberland, not having touched a brush for some time before we left London, and I found it a pleasure to watch a picture growing under his hand – from the first warm ground that was made to cover the canvas before his subject was begun, to the last indefinable change in one of his women's faces, cold in their loveliness, unsubstantial in their passion, tainted with the melancholy that clings perhaps to the purest beauty. Naturally, he had no models, and speaking of that drawback, he said:

"It's wonderful what a bit of nature will do for you when you can get it in"; but he also said something about style being injured by a slavish submission to fact.

I remember that I asked him what was the reason he had never painted the great dramatic compositions he had designed in earlier years – the "Hamlet", the "Cassandra", and, above all, the "Mary Magdalene at the Door of Simon the Pharisee" – the designs in my rooms at Chelsea. He answered with a laugh:

"Bread and butter, my boy, that was the reason. I had to paint what I could sell. But I'll tell you something," he added quickly; "I like best to paint a picture that will boil the pot, yet be no pot-boiler."

The days were already short, the nights were long. Rossetti could not read with ease by lamplight, or sleep until the small hours of the morning; and so it came about that during our first cheerful weeks in

Cumberland he threw himself with great ardour into my own occupations. I was still preparing my lectures on prose literature, and to fortify myself for my work I was reading the masterpieces over again. Seeing this, Rossetti suggested that I should read them aloud, and I did so.

Many an evening we passed in this way. It lives in my memory both as a sweet and a sad experience. Behind our little farmhouse was the lowest pool of a ghyll, and the roar of the falling waters could be heard from without. On the farther side of the vale there were black crags where ravens lived, and in the unseen bed of the dale between lay the dark waters of Thirlmere. The surroundings were impressive enough to eye and ear in the daylight; but when night came, and the lamps were lit and the curtains were drawn, and darkness covered everything outside, they were awesome and grim.

I remember those evenings with gratitude and some pain – the little, oblong sitting-room, the dull thud of the waterfall like distant thunder overhead, the crackle of the wood fire, myself reading aloud, and Rossetti in his long sack-coat, his hands thrust deep in its upright pockets, walking with his heavy and uncertain step to and fro, to and fro, laughing sometimes his big, deep laugh, and sometimes sitting down to wipe his moist spectacles and clear his dim eyes. Not rarely the dead white gleams of the early dawn before the coming of the sun met the yellow light of our candles as we passed on the staircase, going to bed, a little window that looked up to the mountains and over them to the east.

Perhaps it was not all pleasure, even so far as I was

concerned, but certainly it was all profit. The novels we read were "Tom Jones", in four volumes, and "Clarissa" in its original eight, one or two of Smollett's, and some of Scott's. Rossetti had not, I think, been a great reader of English fiction (French he knew better), but his critical judgment on novels was in some respects the surest and soundest I have ever known. Nothing escaped him. His alert mind seized upon everything. He had never before, I think, given any thought to fiction as an art, but his intellect played over it like a bright light. It amazes me now, after forty years' close study of the methods of story-telling, to recall the general principles which he seemed to formulate out of the back of his head for the defence of his swift verdicts.

"Now why?" I would say, when the art of the novelist seemed to me to fail in imaginative grip.

"Because so-and-so must happen," Rossetti would answer.

He was always right. He grasped with masterly strength the operation of the two fundamental factors in the novelist's art – the sympathy and the "tragic mischief". If these were not working well he knew by the end of the first chapters that, however, fine in observation, or racy in humour, or true in pathos, the work as an organism must fail.

It was an education in itself to sharpen one's wit on such a grindstone, to clarify one's thought in such a stream, to strengthen one's imagination by contact with a mind that was of "imagination all compact". But how did Rossetti, who had spent his energies on two other arts, know the things that are hidden for all time from nine-tenths of the self-appointed professional guides to fiction? What explanation is possible, except the one I have given before, that Rossetti was the one man I ever met who gave me a sense of the presence of a gift that is above and apart from talent – in a word, genius.

Down to that time, when I was beginning to live in the outer courts of literature as a lecturer and an occasional reviewer on the two leading literary journals, *The Athenaeum* and *Academy*, it had never occurred to me that I might write a novel. But I began to think of it then as a remote possibility, and the immediate surroundings of our daily life brought back recollections of certain Cumbrian legends told to me by my maternal grandmother. I told one of the stories to Rossetti. He was impressed by it, yet he strongly advised me not to tackle it, because he saw no way of getting sympathy into it on any side.

"But why not try your hand at a Manx story?" he said, remembering my Manx origin. "The Bard of Manxland – it's worth while to be that."

I thought so, too, and hence Rossetti was in some sort the foster-father of the novels with which, perhaps, more than any other efforts of mine, my name has since been associated.

Rossetti was not one of the people who live over and over again the lives they lived in their youth, but during those first cheerful weeks in Cumberland, prompted thereto by my inquiries, he talked a good deal in an easy and familiar way about the men and women he had known in earlier years. They pass before me now, as they appeared in Rossetti's graphic sketches, these people of the world he used to live in, some of them grim and lugubrious forms, slightly dis-

torted by caricature; others, rather rakish young
figures out of the borderland of a somewhat boisterous Bohemia.

Not to charge Rossetti too strictly with responsibility for what comes back to me across the space of so
many years, I will give a summary of his reminiscences. Thus he talked of George Eliot, then lately
dead, with her long, weird, horsey face, a good
woman, modest, retiring and amiable to a fault when
the outer crust of reticence had been broken through.
Then of her companion, Lewes, with his shaggy eye-
brows, and of how, at George Eliot's request, he had
sent a photograph of his "Hamlet" when Lewes, who
was a kind of amateur actor, was about to play the
part. Then he talked of Mrs. Carlyle (how much he
knew of her I cannot remember), as a clever, but
rather bitter little woman, with the one redeeming
quality of unostentatious charity. "The poor of Chelsea always spoke well of her," he said. Then of Carlyle
himself, with a tinge of personal dislike, telling how
Bell Scott sent the Seer his first volume, "Poems of a
Painter", a title which, being written in florid lettering
of the poet's engraving, was mistaken for "Poems of a
Printer", and called forth a letter beginning: "If a
Printer has anything to say, why in the name of
heaven doesn't he *say* it, and not sing it?" Then of
Scott walking with Carlyle on the Chelsea Embankment and pouring out his soul in a rhapsody on Shelley until the grim philosopher stopped him and said:
"Yon man Shelley was just a scoundrel, and ought to
have been hanged" – a crushing blow which was
atoned for a few hours afterwards, when there came as
a present to Scott's house, from Carlyle's, the bust of

Shelley which had been made by Mrs. Shelley, and given to Leigh Hunt. Finally, of Carlyle walking with William Allingham in the neighbourhood of the Kensington Museum, and announcing his intention of writing a life of Michael Angelo, and then adding, by way of remonstrance against his companion's quickening interest: "But, mind ye, I'll no say much about his *art*."

He talked of Browning, too, claiming to be one of the poet's first admirers, and describing him, as I afterwards saw him, spruce, almost dapper, wearing gloves that seemed to have grown on his shapely hands, more than hinting that, perhaps, he gave himself up too much to society, and saying: "Dull dogs for the most part, those fasionable folk, yet they treat a man of genius as if he were a superior flunkey." He talked of Elizabeth Barrett Browning, too, with respect amounting almost to reverence. Of Tennyson, also, he talked with warmth, imitating the sonorous tones of his glorious voice, but betraying a certain soreness at the recollection that to avoid giving an opinion on the "Poems", the Laureate had merely acknowledged the arrival of the book. Then he told a story of Longfellow, "the good old bard"; how the poet had called on him during his visit to England, and been courteous and kind in the last degree, but having fallen into the error of thinking that Rossetti the painter and Rossetti the poet were different men, he had said, on leaving the house:

"I have been very glad to meet you, Mr. Rossetti, and should like to have met your brother, also. Pray tell him how much I admire his beautiful poem, 'The Blessèd Damozel.'"

"I'll tell him," Rossetti had said.

Rossetti's talk about Ruskin was, I thought, curiously contradictory in tone and feeling, being sometimes tender, generous, highly appreciative, and warmly affectionate, and sometimes grudging and even hostile, as when, in reply to something I had said about a difference with Madox Brown on the subject of Ruskin's economic propaganda, he said:

"Brown is one of the most naturally and genially gifted talkers I know, but that mention of yours of the biggest of all big R's (Ruskin) was just the unluckiest thing you could have said. And I myself think that the talk from and about that particular Capital Letter is already enough for several universes, only don't say I said so, as he is an old acquaintance."

If, after so many years, both Rossetti and Ruskin being dead, I disregard the warning of these last words, it is only to say that always in the talk of the one about the other there was this note of desire to avoid the appearance of disloyalty to a friend of former years, who was a friend no longer. I should have said that there had been a short period in which Ruskin and Rossetti had been on terms of the closest intimacy, and that an estrangement had followed that was due merely to that gradual asundering which is more fatal to friendship than the most violent quarrel. The period of intimacy had apparently covered the most tragic moment of Ruskin's life, for I recall a story which Rossetti told of the dark days of his friend's marriage and separation.

Ruskin and his wife had gone up, I think, to Scotland, and there Millais had joined them, with the object of painting a picture. The picture represented the author and his young wife standing at the foot of a waterfall; and when it was finished it became Ruskin's property, and he took it back with him to London. Then the storm-cloud burst, which separated Ruskin from his wife, and gave her to his friend, whereupon Ruskin's father, thinking he saw in the portrait of his son the first indications of a malign intent, wished to put his penknife through the picture. But Ruskin himself, whose love of a work of art was greater than his hatred of the artist, smuggled the incriminating canvas into a cab, and carried it off to Rossetti's studio, begging that it should be hidden away until his father's anger had cooled.

Brighter and better, however, because more easy and familiar than Rossetti's talk of the people who had stood a little apart from him, were his sketches of his own particular circle in the days of their beginnings in art and literature, when all the world was young: of Swinburne, with his small body and great head, full of modern revolutionary fire and the courage of an ancient morality, whereof his personal conduct was as innocent as a child's; of Burne-Jones, with his delicate face and eyes that were alight with dreams – a strong soul in a frail body, a sword too keen for the scabbard; of Morris ("Topsy" he called him), with his rather rugged Scandinavian personality, writing some the "Earthly Paradise", I think, at Cheyne Walk, and declaiming it aloud from a balcony at the back, to the consternation of the neighbours who saw a shock-headed man shouting at nothing in the garden below; of Millais, something of a "swell"; of Holman Hunt, more humbly born, with himself in a social condition somewhere between; of Madox Brown, with his sense of personal dignity and his respect for the proprieties sometimes outraged by Rossetti's utter disregard of appearances, as when, out together in Holborn, Rossetti stopped at a potato-stall on the pavement, bought two-pennyworth of roasted potatoes, and ate them as he walked along, while Brown, in high dudgeon, walked parallel with him on the other side of the street, so as not to be dishonoured by his companionship.

Then there were Rossetti's sketches of the bright days at Oxford, when the group of young artists were painting the frescoes in the Union debating-room, being always in want of female models, and daily discovering "stunners", particularly in one to whom I have referred as belonging to the innermost circle of the best and purest influences on his life. And finally, there were faint glimpses of almost fatal flirtations on that borderland of a rather boisterous Bohemia, when Rossetti, in his tumultuous youth, walking in Vauxhall Gardens, came upon a bouncing girl, fresh from the country, with a great mass of the red hair he loved to paint, cracking nuts with her white teeth, and throwing the shells at him.

There was no meanness in Rossetti's stories – nothing that even for a moment made you squirm. His memory, naturally a generous one, had hoarded up no ugly story to the disadvantage of friend or foe. Blunt, bluff, perhaps occasionally brutal, his summary of a former acquaintance might be, but it was never for an instant cruel or small. And if he was sometimes frank about others, he never spent any pains in painting up a flattering picture of himself. His own portrait, as he left it on my mind in his rapid sketches of early days,

was that of a masterful young man, a little selfish perhaps, certainly domineering, moving in a group of
friends who yielded to him or got out of his way, but
never struggled with him or fought for supremacy –
the portrait, in short, of the spoiled child of his circle.

He was not fond of telling stories against himself,
being intensely sensitive to ridicule, but he could on
occasion laugh at his own expense. One story he told
was of his childish conduct with a dangerous medicine. It was a preparation of, I think, strychnine, and
he had to take four doses a day: the first on rising, the
second at noon, the third in the evening, and the last
on going to bed. Having an engagement to lunch out
of London one day, he was on the point of leaving the
house when he remembered that he had not taken his
medicine, and returning to the studio he took the dose
that ought to have been taken in the morning. He was
again on the point of leaving when he remembered
that a second dose was due, so he went back and took
that also. Once more he was on the point of going
when he reflected that before he could return home a
third dose might be overdue, so, to meet contingen-
cies, he took that as well. Fully satisfied that he had
now discharged his duty, he sailed out of the house,
but before he had gone far he found his hands twitch-
ing and his legs growing stiff, whereupon he remembered what his medicine had been, and becoming
frightened, he looked out for a cab to take him to the
doctor. No cab being anywhere in sight, he began to
run in the direction of the nearest cab-rank, and from
exercise and terror together he was soon in a flood of
perspiration, which relieved his symptoms and carried
off the mischief.

Another story Rossetti told against himself was of a purchase he had been compelled to make by reason of a little boyish bravado. Going one day with some of his artist friends to a tavern, I think in Soho, he came upon an oil-painting of the crudest colour and most hideous design, so huge as to cover the whole side of a room, and so grotesque in subject that they all burst into roars of laughter at the sight of it. Such unseemly merriment nettled the tavern-keeper, who began to remonstrate, to tell them what a work of art the picture was, and what store he set by it.

"Well, well," said Rossetti, with a wink all round, "how much will you take for it?"

"More money than you've got in the world, young man," replied the tavern-keeper; and then, Rossetti, now nettled in his turn, said:

"Really! We'll see. Say the word – how much?"

"Five hundred pounds," said the tavern-keeper.

Then the young painters burst into screams of laughter, Rossetti's laughter being loudest of all. The tavern-keeper stood quiet and silent until they were finished, and then said to Rossetti:

"Well, young man, how much will you give for it?"

"Five *shillings*," said Rossetti.

"Done," said the tavern-keeper, "take it away at once."

I think I afterwards saw the picture for myself in the long dark corridor to Rossetti's bedroom at Cheyne Walk.

Again, another of Rossetti's stories, dating from the days of his tultuous young manhood, was of a ridiculous prank in the manner of the one told of Shelly, who got rid of the old woman with an onion basket in the stage-coach by seating himself on the floor, fixing a woeful look upon his companion, and saying, in thrilling tones:

"For heaven's sake, let us sit upon the ground
And tell sad stories of the death of kings."

Rossetti's frolic had been akin to this, though the results had been amusingly different. In early years, when William Morris and Burne-Jones shared a studio, they had a young servant maid whose spirits were unquenchably vivacious, and whose pertness nothing could banish or check. Thinking to frighten this girl out of her complacency, Rossetti, calling one day on his friends, affected the direst madness, strutted ominously up to her with the wildest glare of his eyes, and began in his most sepulchral tones to recite the lines:

"Shall the hide of a fierce lion
Be stretched on a couch of wood,
For a daughter's foot to lie on,
Stained with a father's blood?"

The poet's response is a soft "Ah, no!" but the girl calmly fixed her eyes on the frenzied eyes before her, and answered, with a swift, light accent and a merry laugh:
"It shall, if you like, sir!"
Pale phantoms of the figures that floated through Rossetti's stories of these earlier years, how they rise around me! And if I present them now, nearly half a century afterwards, it is as witnesses to the cheerful mood of the poet during those first weeks in Cumberland, rather than as wraiths to be challenged too

literally after moving in my memory through so many years.

The change of air and scene had apparently made the most astounding improvement in Rossetti's health, and we began to encourage hopes of a complete recovery. It was a splendid dream, full of great possibilities for the future. After all, he was only fifty-three years of age, and he had a world of work in his heart and brain which he had hardly attempted to achieve. Thus we nourished our glorious hopes, and I think there were moments when even Rossetti himself appeared to share them.

CHAPTER XII

LAST WEEKS IN THE VALE

Our dream was not to be realized. After a while Rossetti's physical vigour became sensibly less, and his spirits declined rapidly. He painted very little, and made no attempt to write the ballad which he had spoken of as likely to grow in the midst of our romantic surroundings. I think now that perhaps these surroundings themselves had some effect in lowering the condition of his health. Exhilarating and inspiring as the scenery of the Lake country certainly is in the cheerful days of summer, it is depressing enough when the leaves fall and the bracken withers and the deepening autumn drives long dun-coloured clouds across the valleys, cutting off the mountain tops and deadening the air as with the daily march of noiseless thunderstorms. And Rossetti seemed to feel the effect of the dying year in a country which gives one the sense of being shut in by mountain and cloud.

Once a week I had to leave him for a day and a half to fulfil my lecturing engagement in Liverpool, and the increasing earnestness with which the reticent Cumbrian dalesman, who always met me on my return, with a dogcart at the station, used to say, "you'll be welcome back, sir," told me but too plainly that

Rossetti's health and spirits were sinking.

Week after week I brought back great stories of how the world was ringing with his praises, but save for a momentary emotion, betraying itself in a certain tremor of the voice as he said, "That's good, very good." I saw no sign of real interest in his growing fame, certainly no heartening and uplifting effect produced by it.

I tried in vain to interest him in the literary associations of the district. It was, perhaps, natural that Grasmere could not draw him, even though he could think of Dove Cottage not only in connection with Wordsworth (whom he did not worship), but also with De Quincey and that Oriental opium-eater who, perhaps, wandered out of a distempered imagination into that secluded dale. I could not get him to go with me to Keswick, only five miles away, to look at Greta Hall, sacred to the memory of Southey's stainless life; or to the cottage on Castlerigg, where Shelley ("as mad there as anywhere else, madder he could not be," as Rossetti said) struggled with the burglars and chased the ghosts; not even Borrowdale, the supposed scene of the second part of "Christabel", could draw him to the cliffs that had been rent asunder in the passage he liked best of the poet he admired most.

Even his daily walks became shorter day by day, sometimes as far as to the Nag's Head on the south, or the mouth of the valley road on the north; but generally no more than a few hundred yards along the highroad to right or left, ending too frequently in a long rest on the grass, however damp from dew or rain.

If Rossetti's days were now cheerless and heavy,

what shall I say of the nights? At that time of the year the night closed in as early as seven o'clock, and then in that little house among the solitary hills, his disconsolate spirit would sometimes sink beyond solace into irreclaimable depths of depression. Night after night we sat up until eleven, twelve, one, and two o'clock, watching the long hours go by with heavy steps, waiting, waiting, waiting for the time at which he could take his first draught of chloral, drop back on to his pillow, and snatch three or four hours of dreamless sleep.

In order to break the monotony of such nights Rossetti would sometimes recite. His memory was marvellous. I have never known anything like it. Thus, at my request, he would again and again repeat his great "Cloud Confines", or stanzas from "The King's Tragedy" or "The White Ship" or "Jenny".

"Rossetti," I would say, "I do believe you could recite every line you have ever written."

"I really believe I could – everything I have ever published, anyway."

It was true. And not everything of his own, merely, but every sonnet of Shakespeare and of other Elizabethans, as well as many of the early Italian poets. His memory was exact, too; not like that of most of us (my own in particular) slack and broken, retaining the substance but missing the word. In moods of depression he would repeatedly recite from Poe – "Ulalume" or "The Raven";

> " 'Twas then the moon sailed clear of the rack,
>   On high in her hollow dome."

I can still hear the deep boom of his baritone rumbling

in our narrow room like an organ. I can hear, too, the panting breath that followed such exertions, when he stopped in his perambulations to and fro and sank into a chair.

It was, perhaps natural enough that in this condition of health and spirits, amid surroundings which I now see were entirely wrong for him, though I had been chiefly responsible for them, the craving for the chloral should increase. Not soon shall I forget some of my experiences in that relation, and if (following the example of De Quincey and Coleridge) I tell the story of one of them, and for the last time lay bare the infirmity (already well known and much misunderstood) of the great man who was my intimate friend, it shall only be to show how the noblest nature may be corrupted, the largest soul made small, by indulgence in a damnable drug.

I have said that on the night I first slept at Cheyne Walk, Rossetti, coming into my room at the last moment before going to bed, told me that he had just taken sixty grains of chloral, that in four hours he would take sixty more, and four later yet another sixty. Whether there was a conscious exaggeration, or whether (being incapable of affectation or untruthfulness) he was deceived by his doctors for the good purpose of operating to advantage on his all-potent imagination, I do not know; but I do know that when the chloral came under my own control I was strictly warned that one bottle at one dose was all that it was necessary or safe for Rossetti to take. This single bottle (by Dr. Marshall's advice) I gave him on going to bed, and we made the hour of retiring as late as possible, so that when he awoke it might be day.

But the power of the dose was now decreasing rapidly, and hence it came to pass that towards four o'clock in the leaden light of early dawn Rossetti would come to my room and beg for more. Let those who never knew Rossetti censure me, if they think well, for yielding at last to his pathetic importunities. The low, pleading voice, the note of pain, the awful sense of a body craving rest and a brain praying for unconsciousness, they are with me even yet in my memories of the man sitting on the side of my bed and asking for my pity and my forgiveness.

These were among the moments when Rossetti was utterly irresistible, but to compromise with my conscience I would give him half a bottle more, and he would go off with an appearance of content. The result was disastrous enough, but in a way that might have been least expected.

I was already painfully aware of the corroding influence of the drug on Rossetti's better nature, and one morning, as I took out of its hiding-place the key that was to open the glass doors of the little cabinet which contained the chloral, I caught a look in his eyes which seemed to say that in future he would find it for himself. To meet the contingency, and at the same time to test a theory which I had begun to cherish, that the drug was only necessary to Rossetti because he believed it to be so, I decided to try an experiment, and so defeat by a trick the trick I expected.

The solution of chloral was hardly distinguishable at any time from pure water, and certainly not at all in the dead white light of dawn, so, with the connivance of the nurse, I opened a bottle, emptied it of the drug, filled it afresh with water, corked and covered it again, with its parchment cap tied about by a collar of red string, placed it in the cabinet, and then awaited results.

Next morning I awoke of myself exactly at the hour at which Rossetti had been accustomed to awaken me, and I heard him coming as noiselessly as he could down the corridor towards my room. He opened the door, leaned over me to satisfy himself that I was asleep, fumbled for and found the key to the cabinet, opened it, took away the bottle I had left ready for him, and then crept back to bed. After some ten minutes or more I rose and went to his room to see what had occurred; and there, sure enough, lay Rossetti, sleeping soundly, and my bottle standing empty on the table by his side.

In my ignorance I imagined I had solved the problem of Rossetti's insomnia (of nearly all insomnia), and found the remedy for half the troubles of his troubled life. He was indeed "Of imagination all compact", and if we could only continue to make him think he was consuming chloral while he was really drinking water, we should in good time conquer his baneful habit altogether.

What the result might have been of any consistent attempt to put my theory into practice it is not possible for me to say, for fate was stronger than good intentions, and my experiment was not to be repeated. While I was out walking the next morning the nurse, taking the liberty of an old friend, told the whole story of what I had done to Rossetti in a well-meant, but foolish, attempt to triumph over his melancholy, and then more mischief was done than the mischief I had tried to undo.

Besides the crushing humiliation that came to him, as to De Quincey, with the consciousness of the lowering of his moral nature from the use of the drug, and of our being so obviously aware of it, there was the fact that from that day forward he believed I was always deceiving him, and that what I gave him for chloral was mainly water. As if to establish my theory that Rossetti's body answered entirely to the mood of his mind, sleep, from that day forward, refused to come to him at all after the single bottle which the doctor had permitted me to give him. Then the dose had of necessity to be increased, and when, in alarm at the consequences, I refused to go farther, Rossetti (with the help of the person I have spoken of, but unknown to me) resorted to other aids to induce the sleep that chloral of itself would not bring.

If I could bring myself (which I cannot, even with the best of precedent) to tell the story of what happened next, I think it would not be a matter for surprise that, young as I was, I took a drastic step to save Rossetti from himself and from his evil influences. I was still going to Liverpool to deliver my weekly lecture for the Corporation, and after one of the last of such excursions the old Cumbrian dalesman who met me with his dogcart at the nearest station, gave me his usual salutation with a significant emphasis: "You'll be *varra* welcome to-night, sir."

"What has happened?" I asked.

"The nurse has gone."

I found Rossetti pitifully alone. He received me with a ghostly echo of the cheery "Hulloa" of earlier days, and then asked about my experiences of the night before – what sort of audience I had had, and how my lecture had gone. I rattled on for a while with my customary account of trivial incidents, but it was impossible for me to see that the new condition could not last; and before long it was with unspeakable relief that I heard Rossetti express a desire to go back to London.

Before that could be, however, I was for some little time alone with the poet. Corrspondence he had always kept up with the friends of his immediate circle, with his brother William, with Watts, and, I think, with Shields, and this had brought a constant flow of interests into his life; but now he was becoming more and more dependent upon personal company that should not fail him, and never for an hour could he bear to be alone. Strange enough, it seemed that the man who for so many years had shunned the world and chosen solitude when he might have had society, seemed at last to grow weary of his loneliness. But so it was; and whatever the value of my own company in the days when I came up to him out of the fresh air of a widely different world, I was growing painfully aware that it was very little I could do for him now.

I had tried to check the craving for chloral, but unwittingly I had done worse than not check it; and where the lifelong efforts of older friends had failed to eradicate a morbid, ruinous, and fatal thirst, it seemed presumptuous, if not ridiculous, to think that the task of conquering it could be compassed by a young fellow with heart and nerves of wax. Moreover, the whole scene was beginning to have an effect upon myself that was more personal and more serious than I have yet given hint of. The constant fret and fume of this life of baffled effort, of struggle with a deadly drug that had grown to have a separate existence in my mind as the existence of a fiend, was beginning to make me ill; and utterly disastrous as our visit to Cumberland had been on the whole, and largely to blame as I felt for it, I jumped eagerly at the opportunity of going home.

Many were the preparations that had to be gone through again before we could make a move; easels and canvases to pack, and a special saloon to bring round from the junction to our wayside platform, so that we might go up without a change and at night – above all, at night – to avoid the distraction of day and the eyes of the people on the stations at which the train might stop. But at length, one evening in the gathering darkness, a little more than a month after our arrival, we were back at Threlkeld in a carriage which half-an-hour later was coupled at Penrith to the Scotch express to London.

Never shall I forget that journey.

Whether Rossetti took his usual dose of the drug I cannot remember, but certainly he did not sleep, and neither did he compose himself to rest, though the lamps of the carriage were darkened by their shades. During the greater part of the night he sat up in an attitude of waiting, wearing overcoat and hat and gloves, as if our journey were to end at the next stopping-place; but at intervals he made effort to walk to and fro in the jolting saloon, as it was his habit to do in his own studio.

Hour after hour passed in this way, while the lights of the stations flashed by the curtained windows, and I looked out from time to time to see how far we had gone – how near we were to the end. The night was very long, and Rossetti's spirits were more disconsolate than I had ever known them to be before.

Undoubtedly, there was enough in the circumstances of our return to London to justify the deepest depression. Rossetti had gone to Cumberland solely in the interests of his failing health, and he was returning in far worse condition. The flicker of hope which had come with his first apparent improvement had made the sadness of his relapse more dark. In the light of subsequent events it would be impossible to say that he exaggerated the gravity of his symptoms, but it was only too clear that he thought he was going home to die.

As the hours went on he was full of lamentations, and I was making feeble efforts over the rattling and clanging of the car to sustain the pitiful insincerity of the comforter who has no real faith in his own comforting, for I, too, had begun to believe that the road for Rossetti was all downhill now.

It is not for me, who, by virtue of the closest intimacy, was permitted to see a great and unhappy man in his mood of most vehement sorrow and self-reproach, to uncover his naked soul for any purpose less sacred than that of justifying his character against misinterpretation, or bringing his otherwise wayward conduct and mysterious life within the range of sympathy; and if I go further with the story of this terrible night, it is with the hope of that result and no other – no other in the world.

For what I shall say next there is, so far as I know, no witness except my own memory, and that stands between my soul and the soul of Rossetti alone. But for no lower reason than that of lifting the darkest cloud that hangs over the character of my friend above the common and, I think, vulgar charge that his long enslavement to a pernicious drug was due merely to want of manliness in meeting the world on its own terms, and for the purpose of indicating my belief that it was more probably the sequel to an event of the most tragic kind that can enter into a man's life, I will no longer hesitate to say that during the painful journey from Cumberland he told me that on the night of his wife's death, when he returned to her room from his walk, he found a letter or message addressed to himself lying on the table by her side. I think he said he had not shown that letter to anyone, and that he had never mentioned it before. Of this last fact I cannot be certain, but sure I am that he said that the message had left such a scar on his heart as would never be healed.

Rossetti's words during the hours that followed I cannot, except in broken passages, recall, and, if I could recall them, I should not set them down, so deep was the distress with which they were spoken and the emotion with which they were heard; but I can at least indicate the impressions they left on me then, as a young man who had known no more down to that moment than a few of his other friends of some of the saddest and darkest chapters of his life.

The first of those impressions was that, while the long indulgence in the drug might have broken up his health and created delusions that had alienated friends, it was not that, nor yet the bitterness of malignant criticism, that had separated him from the world and destroyed the happiness of his life. The next of my impressions was that Rossetti had never forgiven himself for the weakness of yielding to the importunity of friends, and the impulse of literary ambition, which had led him to violate the sanctity of his wife's grave in recovering the manuscripts he had buried in it. And, above all, it was my impression that Rossetti had never ceased to reproach himself with his wife's death, as an event that had been due in some degree to failure of duty on his part, or perhaps to something still graver, although in no wise criminal.

Let me not seem to have forgotten that a generous soul in the hours of deepest contrition will load itself with responsibilities that are far beyond its own, and certainly it was not for me to take too literally all the burning words of self-reproach which Rossetti heaped upon himself; but if I had now to reconstruct his life afresh from the impressions of that night, I think it would be a far more human, more touching, more affectionate, more unselfish, more intelligible figure that would emerge than the one hitherto known to the world.

It would be the figure of a man who, after engaging himself to one woman in all honour and good faith, had fallen in love with another, and then gone on to marry the first out of a mistaken sense of loyalty and a fear of giving pain, instead of stopping, as he must have done, if his will had been stronger and his heart sterner, at the door of the church itself. It would be the figure of a man who realized that the good woman he had married was reading his secret in spite of his efforts to conceal it, and thereby losing all joy and interest in life. It would be the figure of a man who, coming home late at night to find his wife dying, probably by her own hand, was overwhelmed with re-morse, not perhaps for any unkindness, any want of attention, still less any act of infidelity on his part, but for the far deeper wrong of failure of affection for the one being to whom affection was most due.

Thus the burial of his manuscript in his wife's coffin was plainly saying: "This was how I loved you once, for these poems were written to and inspired by you; and if I have wronged you since by losing my love for you, the solitary text of them shall go with you to the grave." Thus the sadness and gloom of later days, after the poet had repented of his sacrifice and the poems had been recovered and published, were clearly show-ing that Rossetti felt he had won his place among the English poets only by forfeiting the tragic grace and wasting the poignant pathos of his first consuming re-nunciation. And thus, too, the solitude of his last years – with its sleepless nights and its delusions born of in-dulgence in the drug – was not wholly, or even mainly, the result of morbid brooding over the insults of pitiful critics, but of a deep-seated, if wholly un-necessary sense as of a curse resting on him and on his work, whereof the malignancy of criticism was only one of many manifestations.

In this reading of Rossetti's life there is no room at all for any of the gross accusations of ill-treatment or neglect which have been supposed, by some of his less friendly judges, to have burdened his conscience with regard to his wife. There was not one word in his self-reproach which conveyed to my mind a sense of any-thing so mean as that, and nothing I knew of Rossetti's tenderness of character would have allowed me to believe for a moment that he could be guilty of conscious cruelty. But there was, indeed, something here that was deeper and more terrible, if more spiritual – one of those tragic entanglements from which there is no escape, because fate itself has made them.

All I knew of Rossetti, all he had told me of himself, all he had revealed to me of the troubles of his soul, all that had seemed so mysterious in the conduct of his life and the moods of his mind, became clear and intelligible, and even noble and deeply touching, in the light of his secret as I thought I read it for the first time on that journey from Cumberland to London. It lifted him entirely out of the character of the wayward, weak, uncertain, neurotic person who could put up a blank wall about his existence because his wife had died by the accident of miscalculating a dose of laudanum; who could do a grave act and afterwards repent of it and undo it; who could finally shut himself up as a hermit and encourage a hundred delusions about the world because a rival poet had resented his success. Out of all this it raised him into the place of one of the great tragic figures of literature, one of the great lovers, whose lives as well as their works speak to the depth of their love or the immensity of their remorse.

It has only been with a thrill of the heart and a trembling hand that I have written this, but I have written it; and now I shall let it go to join other such incidents in literary history, because I feel that it is a true reading of the poet's soul, and one that ennobles his memory. I wrote it all, or the substance of it all, with the story of another incident narrated in this chapter, forty-six years ago, but I did not attempt to publish it then from sheer fear of lowering the temperature of reverence in which I thought Rossetti's name ought to

live. But after nearly half a century of conflicting portraiture – much of it very true, some of it very false, all
of it incomplete – I feel that the truth of the poet's life
as it revealed itself to me (or as I believed it revealed
itself to me) can only have the effect of deepening the
admiration and affection with which the world regards
him. The whole truth that hurts is better than the half
truth that kills. And, speaking for myself, I can truly
say that out of the memory of that terrible journey
only one emotion remained, and that was a greater
love than ever for the strong and passionate soul in the
depths of its abased penitence.

It was just daylight as we approached London, and
when we arrived at Euston it was a rather cold and
gloomy morning. Rossetti was much exhausted when
we got into the omnibus that was waiting for us, and
when we reached Cheyne Walk, where the blinds
were still down in all the windows, his spirits were
very low. I did my best to keep a good heart for his
sake as well as my own; but well do I remember the
pathos of his words as I helped him, now feebler than
ever, into his house:

"Thank God! Home at last, and never shall I leave it
again!"

CHAPTER XIII

BACK IN CHELSEA

Very deep and natural was the concern of Rossetti's older friends on seeing how wretched and stricken he looked on his return to London. That going to the mountains instead of to the sea had been a grievous mistake was now apparent to all of them, but the whole extent of the injury sustained was perhaps not at first realized by any.

Attributing Rossetti's physical prostration chiefly to hypochondriasis, they did their best during the next few weeks to induce him to take a hopeful view of life. The cheerfulness of their company, after what I well know must have been the lugubrious character of my own, had for a little while a good effect on Rossetti's spirits; and I will not forbear to say that I, too, welcomed it as a breath of morning air after a long month's lingering in an atmosphere of gloom. The sense of responsibility which in the solitude of the mountains had weighed me down was now divided with the friends who were Rossetti's friends before they were mine.

Foremost among these friends was William Rossetti, and looking back to his devotion to his brother's personal needs during the last months of the poet's life, and thinking of his constant absorption in efforts to sustain and promote the poet's fame snce his death, I doubt if the whole history of literary friendships has any such story of brotherly love and admiration. I have said this before, and now the time has come to say it with all emphasis again.

Then there was Frederic Shields, so different from Rossetti in personal character and temperament, and as far apart from him as the poles in spiritual outlook upon life and death, yet always so faithful to the man, so loyal to the artist, so ready to put aside his own interests at the call of the poet's needs.

And then, above all, perhaps, there was Watts, whose affection for Rossetti and beneficial influence upon him was perhaps the most touching and beautiful thing I had ever witnessed. No light matter it must have been to lay aside one's own cherished life-work and ambitions to be Rossetti's friend and brother at a time like this; but through these dark days Watts was with him to comfort, to divert, to interest, and to inspire him – asking meantime no better reward than the knowledge that a noble mind and nature was thereby relieved from gloom or lifted out of sorrow.

If the poet's spirits had been low while we were in Cumberland, they were all but insupportable during the first weeks after our return to Chelsea. No longer able to work at the easel, and full of apprehension about his failing sight, he began to torment himself with the fear of poverty. There might, indeed, have been good ground for uneasiness on this head if Rossetti had lived; for though he had long earned a large income as a painter he had saved little or nothing, and, knowing this, he sometimes made rather grotesque predictions of absolute want. Out of such moods of despondency (which was not all delusion, for he was often unable to paint or write) he had to be rallied by his friends, each in his different way, and I recall with some amusement and a good deal of emotion certain wild and fantastic efforts by Shields to banish his melancholia, as well as some quiet and touching assurances by his brother: "Gabriel," he said, "if the worst comes to the worst, you will come to my house and stay there as long as either of us lives."

But Rossetti's fear of poverty during the first sad weeks after our return to Chelsea was not so hard to contend with as his dread of death. I should say, as I think of this period, that if there was no longer any passionate longing to live there was certainly, with a settled conviction that death was coming, a great fear of dying. What it was exactly that was going on in his mind, what struggle for mastery between the will-to-live and the will-to-die, with the dread of both, I cannot say, but I would venture the opinion that he was shrinking not only from the thought of pain, but also from that sinking into everlasting night and nothingness which was all that, so far as I could see, death seemed to mean to him then.

Never was I conscious that religious faith relieved his fears, still less brightened with any kind of hope the prospect of that passing and parting which is rest and eternal life. On the other hand, I was often aware that everything was distressing that reminded him of death. Belief in God was always with him – that I can firmly say; but religion in the conventional sense appeared to irritate him, and even the ringing of the church bells on Sunday seemed at this time to give him pain.

Perhaps it was a sign of his fear of death that his mind seemed to be constantly brooding upon it. I remember that one day, opening a drawer of the bookcase under the books, he took out a long thick tress of rich auburn hair, and showed it to me for a moment. What he told me about it I cannot remember; but, indeed, there was no need to tell me anything, for I thought I knew what it was and where it came from. That was one of those hushed moments of life in which silence is sacred, and I will not break it by one further word even now. Rossetti's downward road was marked by many sign-posts that pointed to the past.

In spite of all the tender offices of friends, his health declined day by day, and he began to be afflicted by a violent cough. I noticed that it troubled him most at night after the taking of the chloral, and that it shook his whole system so terribly as to leave him for a while entirely exhausted.

The crisis was pending and, almost sooner than any of us expected, it came. One evening a friend of former years, Westland Marston, the dramatist, came with his son, Philip Bourke Marston, the blind poet, to spend a few hours with Rossetti. For a while he seemed much cheered by their company, but later on he gave certain signs of the uneasiness which I had learned to know too well. Moving restlessly from seat to seat, he threw himself at last upon the sofa in that rather awkward attitude which I have previously described. Presently he called out to me, in great nervous agitation, that he could not move his arm, and, upon attempting to rise, that he had lost power in his leg as well.

We were all startled, but knowing the force of Rossetti's imagination on his bodily capacity, I tried to rally him out of his fears.

"Nonsense, Rossetti, you're only fancying it," I remember to have said, rather foolishly. But, raising him to his feet, we realized only too surely that, from whatever cause, he had lost the use of his limbs.

The servants were called, and with the utmost alarm we carried Rossetti to his bedroom, up the tortuous staircase at the back of the studio, and I remember the intense vividness of his intellect at the moment, and his obvious sense of humiliation at his helplessness in our hands.

The blind poet remained in the studio while we were taking Rossetti to his room, and after this was done he and I hurried away in a cab to Savile Row to fetch the doctor. I recall that drive through the streets at night with the blind man, who had seen nothing of what had occurred, but was trembling and breathing fast. An hour after the attack the doctor was in the house.

It was found that Rossetti had undergone a species of mild paralysis, called, I think, loss of co-ordinative power. The juncture was a critical one, and it was decided that the time had come at last when the chloral which was the root of all the mischief, should be decisively, entirely, and instantly cut off.

It is not for me to give an account of what was done at this crisis. I only know that a young medical man was brought into the house as a resident doctor to watch the case during the absence of the physician-in-chief, and that morphia was at first injected as a substitute for the narcotic which the system had grown to demand.

I recall the many hours in which Rossetti was delirious whilst his body was passing through the terrible ordeal of conquering the craving for the former drug, and the three or four days succeeding in which the two forces seemed to fight like demons for possession of him. During this period his mind had a strange kind of moonlight clearness, with a plain sense of all that was going on, a vivid memory of the friends and incidents of the past, with a desire to write letters to people whom he had not seen for years, yet a total loss of executive faculty of every kind. But the pathetic phase passed, and within a week after the experiment had been begun he awoke one morning calm in body, clear in mind, and grateful in heart.

His delusions were all dead, his intermittent suspicions of friends were as much gone as if they had never been, and nothing was left but the real Rossetti – a simple, natural, affectionate, lovable soul.

And now let me say that while it must have been the most pitiful weakness, not to say the most mistaken tenderness on my part (after all that has been published on the subject), to attempt to conceal an infirmity of Rossetti's mind which has led to much misconception of his character, I feel myself justified in alluding to it, and even dwelling on some of its painful manifestations, for the sake of the opportunity of showing that, coming with the drug that blighted half his life, it disappeared when the evil had been removed.

Perhaps none may say with any certainty to what the use of the drug was due, or what was due to it, thought I have already given my opinion that, like Keats's consumption, it came from a far deeper source than the mental disturbance set up by adverse criticism; but sure I am that the sadder side of his life was ever under its shadow, and that he was a new man on the day when it was over.

CHAPTER XIV

THE LAST OF HOME

As soon as Rossetti was himself again he began to see his friends and relatives – Shields, Madox Brown, Sharp and, of course, Watts, who was with him every day. Some report of his seizure must have appeared in the newspapers, for I recall inquiries from well-known people which I received and answered in Rossetti's name, among them being a letter from Turgenieff, who was, I think, in London, and proposed to call. There were few men then alive whom I myself more ardently wished to meet, but I had to write to tell him not to come.

I thought it strange when I realized how strongly Rossetti's real nature possessed the power of attaching people to his person, that few letters came from the famous men still living who had been his friends in earlier years; but the link with the past was not entirely broken, for Burne-Jones came one evening, with his delicate and spiritual face full of affectionate solicitude, and when I took him into the bedroom he was received with a faint echo of the cheery "Hulloa" which he may have remembered so well.

Rossetti must have looked sadly unlike his former self, although our hearts were now so cheerful about him, for when after a long half-hour the great painter came down fromm the bedroom where I had left the two old friends together, he was visibly moved and at first could scarcely speak. I remember that he and I dined in the studio in the midst of the easels, and that turning to an unfinished picture on one of them he said:

"They say Gabriel cannot draw, but look at that hand. There isn't anybody else in the world who can draw a hand like that."

Christmas Day was now nigh, and Rossetti, still confined to his room, begged me to spend that day with him. "Otherwise," he said, "how sad a day it must be to me, for I cannot fairly ask any other."

I had been invited to dine at a more cheerful house, but reflecting that this was my first Christmas in London and it might be Rossetti's last, I readily decided to do as he wished. We dined alone, he in his bed, I at the little table at the foot of it, on which I had first seen the wired lamp and the bottles of medicine; but later in the evening William Rossetti, with his brotherly affection, left his children and guests at his own house, and ran down to spend an hour with the invalid. As the night went on we could hear from time to time the ringing of the bells of the neighbouring churches, and I noticed that Rossetti was not disturbed by them as he had been formerly.

He talked that night brightly, with more force and incisiveness, I thought, than he had displayed for months. There was the ring of sincerity in his tone as he said he had always had loyal and unselfish friends; and then he spoke of his brother, of Madox Brown, and, perhaps, particularly of Watts. He said a word or two of myself, and then spoke with emotion of his mother and sister, and of his sister who was dead, and how they were supported through their sore trials by religious hope and resignation. He asked if I, like Shields, was a believer; and seemed altogether in a softer and more spiritual mood than I could remember to have noticed before.

With such talk we passed the last of Rossetti's Christmas nights; and on many a night afterwards I spent hours with him in his room. The drug being gone, he was in nearly every sense a changed man, and I remember particularly that there was no more fear of poverty and no painful brooding over death. That any hope such as could be called faith had taken the place of dread I cannot positively affirm; perhaps if I had to give in a word a definition of Rossetti's attitude towards spiritual things, I should say it was then that of an agnostic – not of an unbeliever, but of one who simply did not know. Before the mystery of the hereafter, of the unknown and the unknowable, he seemed to stand silent, perhaps content, certainly without any anxious questioning, any agonizing doubts.

Those hours with Rossetti, when he just emerged from the thraldom of so many years, are among the most treasured of my memories, and I recall the impression I had at the time that much of his conversation was like the stern lamp of a ship which casts its light on the path that is past. Thus one day he said: "To marry one woman and then find out, when it is too late, that you love another, is the deepest tragedy that can enter into a man's life."

No more now than before did he interest himself in

the affairs of the world outside his own walls; and what he called "the momentary momentousness" of many political questions seemed never to stir his pulse for a moment. But there was one great social problem which always moved him to the depths; he had dealt with it in both his arts – as a poet in "Jenny", as a painter in "Found", and perhaps in "Mary Magdalene". It was the age-long problem of the poor scapegoats of society who carry the sins of men into a wilderness from which there is no escape. These pariahs, these outcasts, had a fascination for him always, but it was of a kind that could only be felt by a man who was essentially pure-minded.

"That is a world," he used to say, "that few understand, though there is hardly anybody who does not think that he knows something about it."

On Rossetti it seemed to sit like a nightmare. For the poor women themselves who, after one false step, find themselves in a blind alley in which the way back is forbidden to them, he had nothing but the greatness of his compassion. The pitiless cruelty of their position often affected him to tears. That they had transgressed against all the recognized rules of morality and social order, and were often wallowing in an abyss of degradation, did not rob them of his pity. No human creature was common or unclean. "With our God is forgiveness", and feeling this, Rossetti also seemed to feel that behind the sin of these sinners there was always the immensity, even the majesty, of their suffering.

All this he had put into "Jenny", with its tenderness to the little closed soul of the girl and its passionate denunciation of the lust of man; he had put it into

"Found", with the agony of shame in the face of the woman on her knees and the pathos of the net which confined the calf that was going to slaughter in the country cart; he had put it into "Mary Magdalene", too, in the light, as of an awakening soul, in the eyes of the courtesan when she hears the Master's call; but more touching, perhaps more immediately affecting, than any of these great works (in my view the greatest the world has yet seen on this subject) was the talk of the man himself when, at this most spiritual hour of the period in which I knew him, he would speak of what he believed to be one of the poignant tragedies of human life.

I will not shrink from telling of one act of Rossetti's moral courage at that time, which I have never been able to recall without a thrill of the heart. Somewhere I had met with one of the women of the underworld who seemed to me to have kept her soul pure amid the mire and slime that surrounded her poor body. She was a girl of great beauty, some education, refinement, knowledge of languages, and not a little reading and good taste. Her position had been due to conditions more tragic than the ordinary ones, but she was held to it by the same relentless laws which bound the commonest of her class.

It was a very pitiful example of the tragedy which most deeply interested Rossetti, and when I told him about it he was much affected. But he did not attempt or suggest the idea of rescue. He knew the problem too well to imagine that anything less than complete reversal of the social order could help a girl like that to escape from the blind alley in which she walked alone. The only thing that could be done for her was to keep her soul alive amid all the dead souls about her, and this he tried to do.

Asking me to bring him a copy of his first volume of poems (the volume containing "Jenny"), he wrote the girl's name and his own, with a touching line or two, on the title-page, and told me to give her the book. I did so, and I recall the astonishment and emotion of the poor outcast thing, who appreciated perfectly what it meant to the illustrious poet to send that present to a lost one like her. As far as I can remember, I never saw her again nor heard what became of her; but well I know that the tender grace of Rossetti's act was not lost.

I have one more memory of those cheerful evenings in the poet's bedroom with its thick curtains, its black-oak chimney-piece and crucifix, and its muffled air (all looking and feeling so much brighter than before), and that is of Buchanan's retraction of all that he had said in his bitter onslaught of so many years before. One day there came a copy of the romance called "God and the Man", with its dedication "To an Old Enemy". I do not remember how the book reached Rossetti's house, whether directly from the author or from the publisher, or, as I think probable, through Watts, who was now every day at Cheyne Walk, in his untiring devotion to his friend, but I have a clear memory of reading to the poet the beautiful lines in which his critic so generously and so bravely took back everything he had said:

> I would have snatched a bay-leaf from thy brow,
>   Wronging the chaplet on an honoured head;
> In peace and charity I bring thee now
>   A lily-flower instead.

Pure as thy purpose, blameless as thy song,
　　Sweet as thy spirit, may this offering be;
Forget the bitter blame that did thee wrong
　　And take the gift from me.

Rossetti was for the moment much affected by the pathos of the words, but in the absence of his name it was difficult at first to make him believe they were intended for him.

"But they are, I'm sure they are, and Watts says they are," I went on repeating, until he was compelled to believe.[1]

It was a moving incident, and doubly affecting at that moment, when the poet had just emerged from the long night of so much suffering. And it was fit and meet that Buchanan's retraction should come before it was too late for Rossetti to hear of it; but if I had wanted anything to prove to me that the cloud that had hung over the poet's life was not that of another poet's criticism but a far graver thing, I should have found it in the fact that after the first hour of hearing of the retraction, he never spoke of the matter again.

---

1 To a later edition of the novel, published after I had come to known Buchanan, and told him the story of Rossetti's last days, the novelist and poet added a second and still more touching dedication:

To Dante Gabriel Rossetti
Calmly, thy royal robe of Death around thee,
　　Thou sleepest, and weeping brethren round thee stand –
Gently they placed, ere yet God's angel crown'd thee,
　　My lily in thy hand.
I never knew thee living, O my brother!
　　But on thy breast my lily of love now lies;
And by that token we shall know each other,
　　When God's voice saith "Arise!"

Rossetti talked rarely of the "writing men" whom he considered his enemies, although they declared themselves his friends. But of one such he said: "Beware of the writing man who keeps a diary. He will always get you some day."

I have still another memory of those evenings in the bedroom, and it is to me a very touching one. After some little time, in which Rossetti seemed to regain strength, he got out of bed for a few hours every day; and then we realized that he was not recovering. The partly-stricken limbs had gained power in some measure, but his weakness was obvious, and it was only too clear to everybody that the road for Rossetti was indeed all downhill now.

On the last day of the year, I remember, I found this certainty especially oppressive, from the acute sense one always has of coming trouble as one passes the solemn landmarks of time. I could not stay indoors that night, so I walked about the streets, but I had not counted on the fact that by staying out of the house to avoid painful emotions I was only gathering them up to fall in a single blow the moment I came back.

It was about half an hour after midnight when I returned home, and then, as well as I can remember, Rossetti was alone. The church bells were still ringing their cheerful peal as I stepped into his room, and after a feeble effort at the customary "Hulloa", we wished each other "A Happy New Year".

CHAPTER XV

AT BIRCHINGTON

After a few weeks upstairs, Rossetti was able to get down to his studio; but his strength did not increase; so it was decided that the error of the autumn should, if possible, be repaired, by sending him, late as it was, to the seaside. At that moment a friend of earlier days, Seddon, the architect, offered the use of a bungalow at Birchington, a few miles from Margate, and I was asked to go down and look at the place. I did so, and, coming back, I reported so favourably of the house and the situation that Rossetti determined to move immediately.

There were the same laborious preparations as before, only they were lightened now by Rossetti's calmer spirits; and towards the end of January the poet left his home for the last time. Whether he had any premonitions that this was the fact I cannot say, but whatever the hopes of his recovery cherished by his friends, it was clear enough to me that the poet himself had no illusions. And though he gave no outward sign of regret, I will not doubt that the day was a sad one on which he turned his back on the house in which he had known so much joy and sorrow, the place so full of himself, written all over with the story of his life, the studio, the muffled bedroom, the closed-up drawing-room, the little green dining-room, and the garden now ploughed up and lost.

We travelled in ordinary carriages, taking with us the domestic servants from Cheyne Walk, a professional nurse, and my sister, then a little girl. Though so weak, Rossetti was in good spirits, and I remember that, on getting into the compartment, he tried to amuse the child by pretending that the carriage itself had been built expressly in her and his honour.

"Look here," he said, pointing to the initials on the carpet ("London, Chatham, and Dover Railway," as it was then), "They have even written our names on the floor; L. C. and D. R. - Lily Caine and Dante Rossetti."

It had been a fine and cheerful day when I went down to Thanet to report on the land, but it was a dark and sullen one when I arrived there with Rossetti. Birchington was not a holiday resort in those days, though it was being laid out for its career in that character. It was merely an old-fashioned Kentish settlement on the edge of a hungry coast.

The village, which stood back from the shore the better part of a mile, consisted of a quaint old Gothic church, grey and green, a winding street, a few shops, and a windmill; while the bungalow we were going to live in stood alone on the bare fields to the seaward side, and looked like a scout that had ventured far towards the edge of unseen cliffs. The land around was flat and featureless, unbroken by a tree or a bush, and one felt as if the great sea in front, rising up to the horizon in a vast round hill, dominated and threatened to submerge it. The clouds were low, the sea was loud, the weather was chill, and if Rossetti had been able to act on his first impression of Birchington I think he would have gone back to London immediately.

But next day the sun shone, the air was bright, the skylarks were singing, and Rossetti was more content. Our little house (the only one in Birchington at that time) was homely, too, in its simple way – a wooden building of one story, with a corridor going down the middle, and bedrooms opening to front and back. Rossetti chose a back bedroom that he might hear as little as possible of the noise of the sea.

There was a large drawing-room at the end of the corridor, and there we set up Rossetti's easels, laid out my usual truck-load of books, and otherwise prepared for a lengthy sojourn. Somebody lent us a huge telescope and we put that up also, though there was little to look at along the bleak coast except the bare headland of Reculvers, and nothing on the empty sea except an occasional sailing-ship going up to the Baltic, for the great steamers hardly ever came so near.

During the first weeks of our stay in Birchington, Rossetti was able to take short walks with me every morning (he rose earlier now) along the tops of the chalk cliffs overlooking the rugged shore, and round the road that winds about the church and churchyard. It is not without a trembling of the heart that I remember how often we walked round that churchyard as long as Rossetti was able to walk at all. But though he would lean heavily on a stick with one hand, and as heavily on my arm with the other, the exercise soon proved to be too much for him, for he was growing weaker day by day.

Nevertheless his spirits kept up wonderfully, and

besides painting at intervals, he took to poetical compositions afresh, and wrote (of all things in the world for that moment!) a facetious ballad called "Jan Van Hunks", telling an eccentric story of a Dutchman's wager to smoke against the devil. Rossetti himself had never smoked in his life, I think, but his enjoyment of the Dutchman's agony as he recited or dictated to me, in the drawing-room, some of the stanzas he had composed in bed, made the place ring with laughter.

It was wonderful how sensibly he seemed to us at some moments to improve. Spring was striding on with its gentle step and we had our soft English mornings, when the clear blue air came up as from her bath in the sea, fresh and salt and full of song. At such times Rossetti would sit by the window in the drawing-room and paint a little, and even sing to himself as he painted, then rest awhile and paint and sing again. It was almost enough to make us believe that in our dark forebodings we had been deceived – that the great soul of our friend was really coming back, with all his powers of hand and brain unimpaired, out of the darkness of his storm-beaten night, into the peace and beauty of the dawn. How sweet it was to live, how good to breathe! Unconsciously we found ourselves smiling into each other's faces, going about on tiptoe and even whispering when we met.

But we had our serious and even thrilling moments, too, in that house on the edge of the coast, as when the wind roared around the little place at night, and the light of Reculvers was all that we could see through the blackness of rolling rain-clouds, and we knew that long stretches of the chalk cliffs in front were churning down into the champing sea.

I remember that once in the morning, after a storm, when the sea was calm and the sun was shining, we saw that a foreign ship which had come to an anchor a mile or so outside, had taken fire. We heard a little later that the crew, on taking flight from her, had left behind them the body of a comrade who had died during the night. The incident took hold of Rossetti's imagination. All through the day we watched the burning ship, and at night, when hull and rigging were aflame, and nothing was to be seen but that blazing mass in a circle of glittering light, the sense as of a funeral pyre was so strong on both of us that we sat for hours in the darkness to look at it.

Weak as he was in body, his intellect was as powerful as in his best days, and he was just as eager to occupy himself with my own doings and tryings-to-do. Thus in the evenings he would have me read aloud the articles I was writing for the literary journals, and tell him my first vague schemes for the stories that were on the forehead of the time to come.

It is impossible for me to say how much these stories may owe (of whatever may be good in them) to the sure criticism of his searching mind; but I know, and may be permitted to say, that when later I wrote that section of one of my novels, which describes a man who is cut off from his kind and is alone with his own soul, I was drawing deeply of the well of Rossetti's mind as it revealed itself to me.

He may have been half-way to the other world, but he was still not incapable of a level-headed view of any attempt to get there before one's time, and he made more than a single protest against certain spiritualistic tendencies of mine which were born perhaps of the reading of Swedenborg. I particularly recall the vehemence of his objection to my going to a *séance* to which one of his own earlier friends had invited me, and that the reason he gave was like a speech out of "Hamlet", or a passage from Sir Thomas Browne.

"You must not go," he said decisively.

"Why not, Rossetti? Do you think it's all a fraud, and the spirits do not appear?"

"No; but they're evil spirits – devils – and they're allowed to torment and deceive people."

But even during these first weeks at Birchington, Rossetti was not entirely dependent upon me for society and solace. He was visited at intervals by nearly all the friends of his later years, as well as by some of lifelong standing.

Rossetti's spirits would rally perceptibly on the sight of these friends, and then fall as sensibly when they were gone; but when I remember the lighter moments of these rather heavy days, I cannot forget the visit of one other acquaintance, whom I need not name.

This was the person who had carried out the work of the exhumation of his poems. He had been the companion of earlier days, more reckless and tumultuous days perhaps, as well as days of blank darkness. I had often heard him spoken of as a daring and adventurous creature, whose humorous audacity had overcome nearly all fear of his unscrupulousness.

Beginning life as the secretary, I think, of Ruskin, he had ultimately lived on his wits, doing anything and everything for a living, ingratiating himself into the graces and worming himself into the confidence of nearly all the painters of Rossetti's immediate circle

and making Rossetti, in particular, his conscious victim.

One day this soldier of fortune turned up unexpectedly at our bungalow, and was received with the
utmost cordiality. He was a somewhat battered person, with the face of a whipped cab-horse, but so
clever, so humorous, so audacious, that Rossetti's
flagging spirits were wonderfully awakened by his
visit. I think the poet remarked that the last time they
had met was when his visitor had bought "a tiddy bit
of blue" (blue china) for him.

"And what are you doing now, Charles?" said Rossetti.

"Buying horses for the King of Portugal," said the
soldier of fortune, and then Rossetti laughed until he
nearly rolled out of his seat.

Our visitor stayed all day, telling stories, veracious
and apocryphal, of nearly everybody known to us in
the world, and mentioning to me, in a sort of paren-
thetical aside, that when he was a young man he had
written nearly all Ruskin's early books, which was
probably true enough, since he had almost certainly
copied them from the author's manuscript in those
better days when his fingers had done the work which
was now being discharged by his nimbler wits.

Feeble as Rossetti was at the time, the visit of this
unaccountable being did him good, and he laughed all
evening after the man had gone, talking of his adventures of various kinds, as well as telling his familiar
stories over again. One of the latter, which particularly amused Rossetti, was of a man near to death, to
whom the clergyman came and said: "Dear friend, do
you know who died to save you?"

"Oh, meenister, meenister," said the dying man, "is this a time for conundrums?"

All this, however, was but the flickering of the lamp that was slowly dying out. It was only too obvious that Rossetti's strength was becoming less and less. His eyesight was feebler, and having already given up his attempts to paint, he had now given up his efforts to read. With difficulty he rose for a few hours every day, and only with the help of the nurse's arm or mine was he able to reach the drawing-room. Seeing how things stood with him, I suggested that he should let me send for his mother and sister, and he consented, saying (as he did more than once afterwards):

"Then you really think I am dying? At *last* you think so!"

CHAPTER XVI

THE LAST OF ROSSETTI

Rossetti's mother and sister came at my call without more than a day or two's delay. The mother, a little sweet woman, with a soft face and a kind of pure morning air always about her, very proud to be the mother of a son whose name was then ringing through the world, very sad to see him so surely going before her. The sister, Christina, a woman of great intellectuality, but without a trace of the pride of intellect, a famous poet herself, yet holding her reputation as nothing compared with that of her brother, whose genius, she plainly thought, was to carry on the family name.

To relieve the long hours of the evenings, I borrowed a great batch of novels from a lending library at Margate, and Christina read them aloud in the drawing-room. She as a fine reader, not emotional perhaps, and certainly not humorous, but always vigorous of voice and full of intellectual life. Rossetti was interested in nearly everything that was read to him, and though some of it was poor stuff, some of it, like "Henry Dunbar", was good, and a litle of it, like "The Tale of Two Cities", was great. I remember that he was deeply touched by Sydney Carton's sacrifice, and said he would have liked to paint the last scene of it – a sad subject, perhaps, but then nearly all great art is sad.

Thus February slid into March, and spring began to come with its soft sunshine and the skylarks singing in the morning, but Rossetti's health did not improve. The hours in the drawing-room became shorter every day, and we all knew that the end was drawing on. At the request, I think, of the London physician, we called in a local doctor, a country practitioner of more than average intelligence, who knew nothing however, of his patient, and asked him some awkward and rather gawkish questions. I remember that one morning I met the good man coming out of the house with a look of confusion on his face, and that he drew me aside and whispered, by way of warning, his secret opinion of the state of Rossetti's mind.

"Your friend does not *want* to live," he said. "If I were to leave a glass of something on the table by his bed, and say, 'Drink that and you'll be gone in five minutes,' it would be done before I could get out of the room."

I thought then the doctor was wrong, and I still think so. True, that by this time the longing for life was gone, and gone, too, was "the muddy imperfection" of fear of death; but quite apart from the restraining sense of the pain he would inflict on his mother and sister, I cannot believe that by any act of his own he would have hastened his end. He was in no pain, he had reconciled himself to the thought that his active life was over, and he was clearly biding his time.

The local clergyman came, too, at Christina's suggestion, I think, and Rossetti saw him quite submissively. He was a fairly capable man, I remember, and when he talked in the customary way of such good souls, Rossetti listened without resistance, having no theological subtleties to baffle him with; but, after a while, the deep, slow, weary eyes of the poet, looking steadfastly at him, seemed to silence the clergyman, and he got up and went away.

Rossetti's attitude towards the other life seemed to be the same then as his attitude towards this life – the attitude of one who is waiting.

> Still we say as we go,
>   'Strange to think by the way,
> Whatever there is to know,
>   That shall we know one day'.

One morning, more than usually cheerful with signs of the coming spring, the local doctor made the painful and somewhat belated discovery that Rossetti was in an advanced stage of Bright's disease, and we telegraphed to his brother, to Watts, and to Shields to come down immediately. That night his dear old mother and I remained with him until early morning, and then his sister took our place by his side.

Since the coming of his mother and sister I had seen less of Rossetti than before, feeling a certain delicacy in intruding upon the sacred intimacies of the home circle in these last reunions; but the next morning, after he had received what we believed to be his death warrant, I spent a long hour alone with him.

"Hulloa! Sit down! I thought at one time you were going to leave me," he said as I went into his room.

"You'll have to leave me first, Rossetti," I replied.

"Ah!"

And then I knew what I had said.

I found his utterance thick and his speech from that cause hardly intelligible, but nevertheless he talked long and earnestly.

He spoke of his love of early English ballad literature, and how he had said to himself when he first met with it, "there lies your line"; and then in a simple, natural way, but with a certain quiet exaltation, reminding me of Keats's calm confidence, he spoke of holding his place among the English poets after his death. After that he half-sang, half-recited snatches from one of Iago's songs in *Othello*.

"Strange thing to come into one's head at such a moment," he said. I had never seen him more bright.

I told him that Watts was on his way, and would be there as fast as the train could bring him.

"Then you really think I am going?" he said.

It was my last interview with Rossetti, alone, of the many I had had of many kinds and I will not shrink from telling the story of the end of it, so deeply does it touch me as often as it comes back to my mind. There had been a friend of his earlier years whom we, of his later life, could not but consider an evil influence. I have already spoken of this friend in another character, so I have little more to say about her now than that Rossetti met her first in the tumultuous days of his early manhood, before his marriage, and that their intimate friendship had long since ceased. Nevertheless he had not permitted himself to forget his old friend in what he believed (I thought quite wrongly) to be her hour of need. After she left us, at a cruel moment, I thought, in the Vale of St. John we had seen no more of her until we were on the point of our departure for Birchington. By this time I had come to share the feeling of Rossetti's older friends that she was still an injurious influence and, taking much upon myself, I had shown her to the door. I believed Rossetti knew I had done right, yet I feared he would never forgive me. But on this last morning alone with him, as I sat by his bed, he whispered:

"Have you heard anything of – ?"

"Nothing at all."

"Would you tell me if you had?"

"If you asked me – yes."

"My poor –," he murmured, and unable to say any more I went out of the room, feeling how poor and small had been our proud loyalty compared with the silent pathos of his steadfast friendship.

On Thursday, April 6, I wrote to his dictation two sonnets called *The Sphinx* to accompany a design of his own. Even down to that time his mind was a clear as sunlight.

Next day (it was Good Friday) the friends we had sent for arrived – his brother, Watts, and Shields, Weak as he was, he was much cheered by their company; but well we knew that he was always aware that the gathering of his friends about him meant that the wings of death seemed to us to be gathering too.

He made his will the day following, leaving everything to his own, with the provision that four of us who had been closest to him during his last years (and one other) should each choose something out of his house to remember him by. Watts drew up the document, I made a fair copy of it; and, after Rossetti had signed it with his trembling hand, it was witnessed by me and by another. Only at that moment did the placid temper of these last days seem disturbed. Money had never been an object in Rossetti's life, and these material provisions seemed to vex him a little now as though they came too late and were dragging his spirit back.

In view of the local doctor's alarming report, the London physician was telegraphed for, and he arrived on Saturday evening. His visit gave great heart to everybody. While recognizing the serious condition, he was not without hope. After examining his patient, he took us all into another room and explained the position. It was true that Rossetti was now suffering from Bright's disease, induced perhaps by the prolonged use of the pernicious drug; but it did not follow that he must die immediately. With care of diet and general watchfulness over the conditions of health, he might still live long. People with that ailment often lived five years, sometimes ten years, even fifteen.

He administered a kind of hot pack, and when I saw him off on Saturday night we were all in great spirits. Next morning Rossetti was perceptibly better, and I think everybody in the house looked in upon him in his room, and found him able to listen and sometimes to talk. It was a beautiful Easter morning, and when the bells rang a joyful Easter peal I think both mother and sister went to church. All was well during the day, and in the evening the nurse gave such a cheery report of the poet's condition that we were very happy. She was about to administer another pack, so we went off to other rooms, the mother and Christina to their bedroom facing Rossetti's, William to the drawning-room, Watts-Dunton, Shields, and I to the dining-

THE LAST OF ROSSETTI

room down the corridor.

About nine o'clock Watts left us for a short time, and when he returned he said he had been in Rossetti's room and found him at ease and very bright. Then we three gave way to good spirits, and began to laugh at little things, as is the way with people when a long strain seems to be relaxed. An instant afterwards we heard a terrible cry, followed by the sound of somebody scurrying down the corridor, and knocking loudly at every door.

We hurried into Rossetti's room and found him in convulsions. Watts raised him on one side, while I raised him on the other. His mother, sister and brother were immediately present (Shields having fled away bareheaded for the doctor); there were a few moments of suspense, and then we saw him pass away in our arms.

Thus, late at night on Easter Day, 1882 at less than fifty-four years of age, Rossetti died. It was all over before we seemed to draw breath. I remember the look of stupefaction in our faces, the sense of being stunned, as we three – Watts, Shields, and I leaving the two good women murmuring their prayers in the death chamber, returned to the dining-room, and said to each other: "Gabriel has gone!"

* * *

Long as we had foreseen the great asundering it fell at last as a surprise. Each of us no doubt had had his vision of how it was to be with Rossetti at the end. In mine he was to die slowly, body and soul sinking gradually to rest, as the boat, coming out of a tempestuous sea, lets fall its sail and glides into harbour. This was to be Nature's recompense for Rossetti's troubled days and sleepless nights; the end of his fierce joys and stormy sorrows. But Nature knew better the mysteries of the future, and Rossetti was to be the same tragic figure to the end, in sunshine and shadow, in life and death, always tragic.

CHAPTER XVII

THE END

William's wife arrived from Manchester a few minutes after Rossetti's death. We agreed that in our small bungalow, already full, a room must be found for her. I gave her mine and proceeded to prepare to sleep on the sofa in the room in which Rossetti lay dead. There was a great outcry against this (I could not then understand why), and in the end a mattress was laid out for me on the hearthrug before the drawing-room fire. As a result I caught a shocking cold which clung to me for weeks. Nevertheless, next morning I plucked some of the big pansies and wild violets that come early in the spring in that fresh sea air; and loving hands laid them on the poet's breast. His face was perfectly placid, the convulsive expression gone; even the tired look that had clung to him in sleep, as the legacy of the troubled years, quite smoothed away. Shields spent the morning in making a pencil sketch of him, finding it a painful task, and weeping most of the time. Later in the day a plaster cast was taken of his head, and also of his small delicate hand. I still possess both the drawing and the cast.

The London newspapers were full of obituary articles, and the drowsy little seaside settlement appeared to awake to some vague consciousness of who it was that had been living in their midst. Nevertheless, I recall the look of blank bewilderment in the face of the local clergyman, who, having come in all gracious neighbourliness to ask where the family wished Rossetti to be buried, meaning in what portion of the churchyard, received William Rossetti's reply in words like these: "If my brother had his due he would be buried in Westminster Abbey."

I wondered why it seemed to occur to nobody that Rossetti should be buried at Highgate with his wife, around whose life (and death) his own life and death had so plainly revolved; but William decided to bury his brother at Birchington, and no doubt he knew best.

I went up to London on some necessary business between the death and the burial; and the gaunt old house in Chelsea, which had always seemed a desolate place to me, for all its wealth of beautiful things, felt more than ever so now that the man who had been the soul of it lay dead in the little bungalow by the sea. I remember the emotion with which I stepped noiselessly into the studio, where there was no longer the cheery voice to greet me; and the sense of chill with which I passed the dark bedroom, now empty, on my way to bed.

I took back from London the feeling that by the death of Rossetti the world had become aware of the loss of a man of two-fold genius, but that its imagination had been most moved by learning of the two or three tragic facts in his storm-beaten life.

The funeral was a private one, and a few of Rossetti's friends came down to it. They were chiefly the friends of his later life, hardly any of the friends of earlier days being there. We heard that Burne-Jones had made an effort to come, and had got as far as the railway station, where he became ill, and turned back. Madox Brown was unwell in Manchester, and Ruskin was now an old man in Coniston; as for the rest, perhaps the time and place of the funeral had not been communicated to them, or perhaps they thought the gradual asundering of the years had left them no right to be there.

It was a dumb sort of day, without wind, and the sky lying low on the sea. When I got into the last of the carriages there were some drops of rain, but they stopped before we reached the church. We were only a little company who stood about the grave, and all I can remember about that group is the figure of the blind poet, Marston, with tears in his sightless eyes. The grave was close by the church porch, and only a few yards away was the winding path where Rossetti and I had so often walked around the place which was now to be the place of his rest.

The friends left us that night, and after a day or two more the family went away. I was ill in bed by this time, and from some other cause Watts also remained a little longer. I thought we two had been drawn closer to each other by a common affection, and the loss of him by whom we had been brought together.

When I was better, and the time had come for us too, to go away, we walked one morning to the churchyard, and found Gabriel's grave strewn with flowers. It was a quiet spring day, the birds were singing, and the yellow flowers were beginning to show. As we stood by the grave under the shadow of the quaint old church, with the broad sweep of landscape in front, so flat that the great dome of the sea appeared to lie on it, and with the sleepy rumble of the rolling waters borne to us from the shore, we could not but feel that little as we had thought to leave Rossetti there, no other place could be quite so fit.

It was indeed the resting-place for a poet. In that bed, of all others, he must, at length, after weary years of sleeplessness, sleep the only sleep that was deep and would endure.